The Visible Library

Practical Public Relations For

BOOKSTORE LOAN

CROOK				
16. OCT 1981				
DARL				
BEL				
6.5.82				
✱				
Co. Hall 3/6				
Bel PETERLEE				
CTON				
21 MAR 1997				
12 Apr 97				
21 Apr 97				

C945425

BOOKSTORE LOAN

COUNTY COUNCIL OF DURHAM
COUNTY LIBRARY

The latest date entered on the date label or card is the date by which book must be returned, and fines will be charged if the book is kept after this date.

In memory of my mother who once climbed a hill.

The Visible Library

Practical
Public Relations
for
Public Librarians

Bob Usherwood

THE LIBRARY ASSOCIATION · LONDON

© Library Association Publishing Ltd 1981.
Published by Library Association Publishing Ltd,
7 Ridgmount Street, London WC1E 7AE.

All rights reserved. No part of this publication may be photocopied, recorded or otherwise reproduced, stored in a retrieval system or transmitted in any form or by any electronic or mechanical means without the prior permission of the copyright owner.

First published 1981

British Library Cataloguing in Publication Data
Usherwood, Bob
　The visible library.
　1. Public relations – Libraries
　I. Title
　021.7　　　Z716.3

ISBN 0 85365 562 6

Printed and bound in Great Britain by Camelot Press, Southampton.
Design and Production Services by Elron Press Ltd., London WC2.

Contents

Acknowledgements x

Preface xii

Part One · The Concept 1

1 What is public relations? 3
2 The objectives of library public relations 9

Part Two · The Communication 17

3 Paper and print 19
4 Audio-visual public relations 37
5 Design and display 47
6 Press relations 57
7 Radio and television 69
8 Public speaking 86
9 Miscellaneous methods 97

Part Three · The Community 111

10 Dealing with people 113
11 Community public relations 126
12 Councillors, councils and committees 138

Part Four · Considerations 155

13	Managing library public relations	157
14	Evaluating library public relations	166
15	Public relations for the library profession	176

Postscript 194

Bibliography 196

Index 201

Acknowledgements

My visit to the United States which provided much of the information included in the following pages was made possible through the receipt of the Senior Librarians Award from the London and Home Counties Branch of the Library Association. I am indebted to the Branch Committee for having faith in my project and I am happy to record publicly my thanks for their support.

Many people in this country and the United States have contributed to this book by means of conversation, demonstration, and cooperation. Any mistakes are mine, as are any opinions expressed, unless attributed. I am glad to acknowledge the help received from the following: Peggy Barber, the American Library Association; John Berry, *Library Journal;* Patricia Boyle, Friends of the Free Library of Philadelphia; Lynne Bradley, District of Columbia Public Library; Carol Bryan; Bessie Bullock, Brooklyn Public Library; Anne Corin, Nottinghamshire County Library; Natalia Davis, Brooklyn Public Library; Joseph Eisner, Plainedge Public Library; Charles Ellis, the Library Association; Bill Eshelman, then with *Wilson Library Bulletin*; Sue Fontaine, Washington State Library; Geoff Ford, Southampton University Library; Dr Franklin, District of Columbia Public Library; Guy Garrison, Drexel University; Gloria Glaser, Nassau Library System; Fred Glazer, West Virginia Library Commission; Terry Hanstock, Sheffield Public Library; Mike Hudson, Sheffield Public Library; James Hunt, Public Library of Cincinnati; Ms Jones, West Virginia Library Commission; Louise Liebold, East Meadow Public Library; Art Milner, Free Library of Philadelphia; Larry Molumby, New York Public Library; Barbara Moro, Chicago Public Library; Cherie Neale; Nick Patselas, Free Library of Philadelphia; Grace Perkinson, Free Library of Philadelphia; Mike Perry, London Borough of Lambeth; the Public Libraries Research Group; Betty Rice; Randall Rosensteel, Free Library of Philadelphia; Ellen Rudley, Brooklyn Public Library; Judy Smith, Suffolk County Library; Edward White, New York Public Library; David Will, the Library Association; Jane Wilson, the American Library Association; E Yungmeyer, the American Library Association.

Over the years we all assimilate ideas from a vast range of sources. I have tried hard to identify those on which I have drawn. I hope that any person who feels that their contribution to the discussion of the topic has been used without due credit will accept my apologies, and my general acknowledgement to the literature of the subject.

Finally, to my wife Hazel, and my children Julie and Tania, grateful thanks for their help, patience and understanding.

The Library Association gratefully acknowledges the use of material published by the American Library Association, Birmingham Public Libraries, Boone-Madison Public Library, Brooklyn Public Library, Chapmanville Public Library, Cincinnati Public Library, City of Coventry Libraries, The Free Library of Philadelphia, Libraries Open and Free (LOAF), Manchester Public Libraries, New York Public Library, Pickens County Library, Plainedge Public Library, Thurman Publishing Limited, The Toy Library Association, West Virginia Library Commission, H W Wilson Co.

Preface

As its title suggests, this is intended as a practical text. However, thought is a necessary prerequisite for successful practice and, while the book is in one sense a 'how to', it also contains some indication as to 'why you should'. Those who wish to refer more fully to the theory behind the practice are invited to make use of appropriate titles listed at the end of each chapter, and in the bibliography. In the future I should like to synthesize the ideas contained in these theoretical works for a library audience. The aim of the present book is to fill the gap in the literature that exists between the simple (but useful) books of PR ideas and the detailed studies on communication and persuasion techniques.

This work develops some ideas obtained during a visit to the United States. However, British libraries operate in a different social, economic, and political context and the book reflects this. In particular, American readers may be surprised to find no special mention of programming — or what British librarians once called 'extension activities'. Lectures, concerts, poetry readings, and the like are an integral part of a service, the purpose of which is the communication of information and ideas.

A library's public relations will of course depend very much on the service it provides. The nature of the book stock, the range of records available, the quality of lectures or concerts will all contribute to the public's view of the library. It is beyond the scope of this work to write in detail about each and every aspect of library service. Its emphasis is on public relations as a management tool for obtaining, retaining, and maximizing resources.

Public relations is an essential part of public library management. At both national and local government level there is a growing realization of the need to promote public library services. To quote the person responsible for the famous, or infamous, vodka advertisement that is still to be found in many library staff rooms: 'librarians have a major PR job to do.' I hope that this book may help public librarians with that task.

BOB USHERWOOD
Sheffield, January 1981

Bookmarks from Brooklyn Public Library

Part One The Concept

'The question of public relations is rarely debated at our meetings . . . If it is incompetently and indifferently done, goodwill, which the committee and the librarian should promote, is diminished.'

Ernest Savage The Librarian and his committee, *1942*

Chapter 1
What is Public Relations?

'Defining public relations is like frisking a seal — you don't come up with much. I've read a hundred definitions of public relations and they're all correct, but none of them is any good. Public relations is a matter of degree, not definition.' Robert B McIntyre.[1]

No organization can avoid having a relationship with its public: such relationships are a fact of organizational life. The function of that part of management known as public relations is to cultivate those relations, so as to improve the good and correct the bad impressions that they create. The objective of this exercise is to influence favourably the attitudes and opinions of those groups and individuals that make up an organization's public. For a public library, those groups could include: national and local legislators, users, potential users, library staff, other council staff, booksellers and other suppliers.

Communicating

The practice of public relations is concerned with the effective management of communications between an organization and such groups. It is a management function 'based on the assumption that public opinion matters'.[2] Public opinion matters because in the final analysis the well-being of any organization may depend on the goodwill of all, or at least some, of the groups and interests that make up its public. Public relations pervades management and it is quite wrong to consider it in isolation from all the other things that go on in an organization. Most things that take place in a library, and some that do not, have a public relations effect. The public librarian, like any other manager, must always seriously consider the PR aspects and implications of the decisions he or she takes.

Public relations should be an integral part of the general management of any organization. PR skills, techniques, and methods can be used to achieve specific management objectives. These may be straightforward aims, such as simply informing the public — or rather its publics — about an institution and the services it offers. Thus, a library's management needs to inform people about such basic things as hours of opening or joining procedures. It also has to tell its staff about conditions of service and other factors that can affect their working lives.

Influencing

In addition to informing, public relations also seeks to influence people. Management, for instance, may use PR to try to persuade legislators to provide additional funding. Over a period of time, good new staff may be attracted to an organization by its reputation. One of the aims of PR is to get people to like you. People who like you are more likely to support you when times get tough. Positive public relations seeks to eliminate the negative aspects of an organization and attempts to reduce people's resistance to a product or service. Thus, information and influence are often linked in a public relations communication. It has been said that 'what you do not know you do not want', and it is certainly one of the major roles of PR to make an organization and its services more widely known and thus more widely used.

Skilfully used, the techniques of public relations can do much to enhance the status of an organization or profession. Increased status may in turn increase the power of that organization or profession to influence public opinion. For public service organizations, public relations communications can be effective in creating a more positive understanding of their value to society. This can lead to a situation in which the community is willing, or at least feels obliged, to give them adequate financial support.

Having suggested a formidable list of things PR can achieve, we should also indicate clearly what it cannot do. Public relations is not a panacea. No amount of public relations activity will win approval for a poor or irrelevant service. If a service organization is to prosper it must provide a good standard of service. Public relations is not a miracle ingredient that managers can simply add to an organization so as to transform a third-rate performance into a first-class one. To suggest that it is, is nonsense.

The image of PR

Perhaps because some of the more unscrupulous practitioners of public relations have sought to make such claims, PR is viewed in some quarters with a degree of suspicion. Its covert nature also worries some people. Indeed, it was not so long ago that Malcolm Muggeridge advocated a law through which public relations people would 'have to identify themselves by means of a badge or tie or better still a clapper or bell such as lepers were forced to wear in the middle ages'.[3]

Ironically, the image of public relations itself is something that continues to worry professionals working in the field. For instance, they take pains to point out that public relations is not propaganda. Most understandably, practitioners want to distance themselves and their work from the kind of persuasion techniques practised in Nazi Germany. They now place some emphasis on the ethical nature of professional public relations. The International Public Relations Association has, for example, adopted codes of professional conduct and ethics, something that, at the time of writing, the Library Association is still trying to achieve.

Although, as long ago as 1926, Edward Bernays was writing that PR had 'developed from the status of a circus agent's stunts' to 'an important position in the conduct of the world's affairs',[4] there is still a tendency to view PR as nothing more than a series of gimmicks. Although gimmicks can occasionally play a part in a public relations programme, to consider PR only in those terms is to undervalue seriously its potential as a productive management tool.

Definitions

It is in fact far easier to describe the practice of PR than to define it. In the commercial world at least, public relations departments make use of the skills not only of journalists and marketing personnel but also those of sociologists, economists, social psychologists, and others with a knowledge of behavioural subjects. The use of such people should not really surprise us because PR is, after all, concerned with human behaviour and with improving communication between people, institutions, and organizations.

Perhaps because of its hybrid nature there are almost as many definitions of public relations as there are writers on the topic. The literature of the subject is full of tortuous arguments about the distinctions between advertising, publicity, and public relations. These need not detain us. Those who do wish to pursue such questions should refer to the books listed at the end of this chapter.[5] Suffice it to say that advertising and publicity are sometimes part of public relations but never a satisfactory definition of it.

A former President of the Public Relations Society of America has explained the role of PR in the following way: 'If a boy tells his girl he loves her, that's advertising, if he tells her how great he is, that's promotion. If her friends tell her how great he is, that's public relations!'[6] Those familiar with the ways of local government in general, and local politicians in particular, might be tempted to add that public relations may also be needed after the event. That is to say there may be times when the boy has to explain why he was not quite as great as he said he was going to be.

Among the more conventional definitions of public relations is that of Edward Bernays, a man who is generally regarded as the father of the modern public relations movement. According to Bernays, public relations is concerned with 'the gaining of public support for an activity, cause, movement or institution'. It is, he says, a process 'that furthers mutual understanding and cooperation between an individual, a corporation, a government, or any organization and its various publics'.[7] The importance of mutual understanding is reflected in the official definition of PR as issued by the Council of the Institute of Public Relations. This states that public relations practice is 'the deliberate, planned and sustained effort to establish and maintain mutual understanding between an organization and its public'.

I would only wish to add an 's' to the last word of that statement to accept it as a satisfactory definition for our specialized purpose. Readers may wish to seek out and refine their own definition of what PR is and, indeed, what it should be. I should, however, be very surprised if the ideas inherent in the words 'communication', 'cooperation', and 'mutual understanding' did not play a significant part in that definition.

More important than a definition of public relations practice is a recognition that public relations exists. Organizational bodies have a state of public relations in the same way that human bodies have a state of health. In the same way that an individual can use various aids and techniques to improve the state of her or his health, so an organization can use skills and strategies to improve the state of its relations with its publics. For the practising manager, the more significant question is not 'what is public relations?' but rather 'what is the condition of my organization's public relations?'

NOTES AND REFERENCES

1 Quoted in *Editor and Publisher* 93 (45), November 1960.
2 Black, S *The role of public relations in management,* Pitman, 1972.
3 Quoted in Barron, C 'The PR paradox', *Management Today,* November 1978.
4 Bernays, E L *Crystallising public opinion,* Boni & Liveright, 1926.
5 The topic has been discussed at some length in the introductory sections of:
Black, S *Practical public relations* 3rd ed., Pitman, 1970, Black, 1972;
Bowman, P and Ellis, N *Manual of public relations,* Heinemann, 1969;
Lerbinger, O and Sullivan, A J *Information, influence and communication,* Basic Books Inc., 1965.
6 Fox, J F 'Worth reading' in Moran, I (*comp.*) *The library public relations recipe book,* Public Relations Section, Library Administration Division, American Library Association, 1978.
7 Bernays, E L 'Public relations' in *Collier's Encyclopedia* 19, Crowell-Collier Educational Corp., 1971.

Chapter 2
The Objectives of Library Public Relations

Every library has relationships with its publics. It is part of the job of the library manager to ascertain the nature of those relationships and to plan and act accordingly. Some possible lines of action are discussed in subsequent chapters but first we must ask, and answer, the question: what are the objectives of library public relations? What are librarians trying to achieve by using methods and techniques previously associated with commercial organizations?

The precise answer to that question will vary from library to library because different libraries will have different priorities, reflecting the needs of their different communities. The emphasis that each library places on the various aspects of public relations may well depend on local circumstances. For instance, one authority may feel that the prime need is to increase the use of a specific service, while another may wish to increase and develop its contact with local institutions. Each library will have specific target groups that it wishes to reach. These will often vary from community to community.

Funding

While it is important to keep such local differences in mind, it is still possible and desirable to formulate some general objectives for public library public relations activities. Many librarians tend to associate library PR first and foremost with increasing the use of library services. This is an important objective but there is a danger that, in concentrating too much on this aspect of PR, the profession will not fully consider the very real role that good public relations can play in achieving resources for library organizations. In order to do this, it is essential to influence favourably public opinion and central and local government attitudes regarding library services. This must be a major objective of any library organization's public relations activities.

As recent history, in both Britain and America, has shown, public libraries need more public support if they are to receive a fair and adequate share of the economic cake. Although the funding situation on the two continents is quite different, librarians on both sides of the Atlantic are having to withstand populist campaigns for cuts in public expenditure. American librarians are having to cope with the after-effects of Proposition 13 and the Jarvis bandwaggon, while in Britain librarians and other public sector workers are faced with a Conservative administration which has an ideological dislike of national or local government expenditure, save that on the police, the military, or private education.

Public library services are then facing increasing competition for decreasing public funds. There is an urgent need for vocal public support. What is required is an effective library lobby. Lord Donaldson, the former Labour Minister with responsibility for libraries, has publicly expressed his regret that such a lobby does not exist, in Britain, at either the national or local level. This is in strict contrast to the quite major lobbies that have been established to put the case for the arts and sport, two areas of activity which, in the United Kingdom at least, are often in direct competition with libraries for local authority funding.

It would, of course, be quite dishonest to suggest that public relations could put an end to all our funding problems. Nevertheless, there are some notable examples of public relations orientated librarians achieving considerable success in budget negotiations. In England, Bill Best Harris, the former City Librarian of Plymouth, estimated that he spent 50 per cent of his time on public relations work. As a result, he maintains that Plymouth was spending more per head on books than almost any other authority in Britain. In the United States, Frederick Glazer, the State Librarian of West Virginia, an aggressive advocate of the hard sell and a self-confessed huckster, has achieved a 50 per cent increase in State funding for library services. In addition, a recent survey of some 37 libraries in the USA has shown that 'libraries that engage in public relations activities ... show higher public support as evidenced by a higher budget allocation than libraries who do not engage in public relations activities'.[1]

Increasing library awareness

Funds, once achieved, are used to maintain, improve, and develop services. It is, of course, important that we encourage more people to use, and to continue to use, the facilities that libraries provide. Public library authorities should then seek to increase the general awareness of their services. Great Britain has one of the finest library systems in the world but how many people really know about it? Why do people still write to magazines or telephone radio stations for information, rather than contacting their local public library? How many library users are fully aware of the vast resources available to them through inter-library cooperation? Indeed, does all the population realise that the basic service is free of direct charges? It is still not an uncommon occurrence for someone to ask as they join a library: 'How much do I pay?' Do we know how many people may be put off joining because they believe a charge is involved? Even if it can be assumed that the indigenous population are aware that the service is freely available, can we be equally sure about newcomers who come from countries without the tradition of a free public library service?

There are those, on the other hand, who are only too aware that the library is paid for through their rates and taxes. However, are they fully aware of the vast range and value of the services they are obtaining for their money? It is a function of library public relations to inform them.

Public image

A significant number of people in the community misunderstand the nature of a contemporary library service. Through library public relations we should seek to establish, develop, and maintain mutual understanding between library organizations and their var-

"Ah" smiled Mr Happy "I have the very job for a quiet chap like you!"

And so, the very next day, Mr Quiet started work.

And he loves it.

Do you know where he works?

In the Happy Lending Library!

As you know, everybody who goes into a library has to be very quiet, and only whispering is allowed.

© *Roger Hargreaves 1978 and published by Thurman Publishing Ltd.*

Catching them young.

ious publics. Image is an overworked word, but there can be little doubt that the general image of libraries and librarianship is not exceptionally good. Perhaps we should not be too sensitive about the stereotyped librarians who continue to appear in television series and the pages of popular novels, but we should realise that they do tell us something about the way that at least some of our public sees us. The man behind the famous or infamous vodka advertisement has said that Smirnoff featured a librarian in their campaign because 'rightly or wrongly, the public at large tend to see the librarian as a person constrained to a boring and humdrum existence',[2] a message reinforced by Roger Hargreaves who, as our illustration shows, sees librarianship as a suitable career for Mr Quiet.

Perhaps more worrying is the fact that there are many people whose perception of public library services is such that they do not see them as being relevant to their everyday lives. Despite the increasing professional awareness of the importance of providing a service to all sections of the community, some people still regard libraries as being for 'them' rather than 'us'. Although there are of course significant exceptions, for too many ordinary working people the public library appears as an irrelevant middle-class institution. As a recent report from the Department of Education and Science states: 'the middle classes, who make up less than a fifth of the population, do account for almost 50% of library membership'.[3]

Internal PR

Sometimes the problem of misperception can be even closer to home. Staff and/or legislators may not always fully understand just what the library service is about. As has already been indicated, the need for the support of councillors in these cost-cutting days is crucial, but staff too should be kept fully informed and encouraged so that they can identify their personal interests with those of the library. It should be emphasized that this should apply to all local authority staff, and not just to those immediately involved in the work of the libraries department. A friend in the Treasurer's office can be a friend indeed. Public relations techniques are therefore required within, as well as without, a library organization. Intelligently implemented, such internal PR can be a very valuable management resource.

Creating confidence

People are more likely to use and support a service in which they have confidence. A further objective of library public relations is then to build confidence in the services a library provides. This can be done in part by eliminating those areas of misunderstanding indicated above but, in addition, it requires that the library management looks critically at the way in which services are provided. It means ensuring that everything the library does is done in the best possible way. It means making sure that every person who works for, or who represents, the library does so in the best possible way. The image of a library is important but in the long run it can never be better than the service the library provides. Public relations has a role to play in establishing the reality as well as the reflection of a library service.

Despite this there will be some in the library profession who will question the whole idea of library public relations. Many in the library world dislike the pre-packaged, cellophane-wrapped world of the public relations man. John Berry, for instance, has argued that an essential public service should not find 'it necessary to peddle its wares as if they were new appliances for a consumer public that is tired of washing dishes, preparing food from scratch, or having hair with split ends'.[4]

In fact, more and more public service organizations are using public relations techniques to put their various messages across. Many local authorities have appointed Public Relations Officers in order to develop good relationships with their ratepayers. Some councils have used design consultants to improve their visual image. These consultants have advised on the design of everything, from public notices and notepaper to staff uniforms and liveries for council vehicles.

None of this is entirely new. From their very earliest beginnings, local authorities strove to give themselves a visual identity. In the early days, this often took the form of a unique and readily identifiable style of architecture. Early libraries were also concerned about their image. It is reported, for instance, that in ancient Thebes the inscription over the library's entrance read 'Medicine for the soul'. At Alexandria the medical imagery was maintained as the library proclaimed itself as a 'hospital for the mind'.

Long before the term public relations was invented, our library forefathers were engaged in promoting library services. They seem to have realised that for a service to develop its full potential, time and effort has to be spent on making it known. What was true in earlier times is even more true today when so many other institutions are competing for the public purse and the public's attention.

REFERENCES

1 Berger, P 'An investigation of the relationship between public relations activities and the budget allocation in public libraries', *Information processing and management*, 15(4), 1979.
2 Quoted in 'In search of a miracle', *Assistant librarian* 65(12), December 1972.
3 Department of Education and Science, *The libraries' choice*, Library information series No. 10, HMSO, 1978.
4 Berry, J 'The selling of the library', *Library Journal* 99(2), 15 January 1974.

Part Two   The Communication

'Libraries in the past have rarely gone in for effective publicity. We think they should be much more prepared to publicise the library in a variety of ways.'

DES The Libraries' Choice, 1978

Chapter 3
Paper and Print

Public libraries produce a wide range of publications. By far the largest percentage of these involves paper and print or at least some form of reprography. The A to Z sequence that follows is not intended as a comprehensive listing of publications but is provided as an indication of the extent of this library activity. Publications can include: annual reports, bookmarks, catalogues, diaries of local events, exhibition catalogues, flyers, guides to the library, house journals, indexes, journals, 'keep out' signs, leaflets, membership forms, newsletters, overdue reminders, postcards, questionnaires, village histories, 'what's on', Xmas cards, year's work, zany ideas.

Finding examples of library publications is not difficult. Since the printed word still plays a significant part in the public librarians' world, it is not surprising that they have sought to use it to serve their own ends. What is surprising is that as 'publishers' librarians have not always applied the same rigorous standards to their own efforts as one would expect them to apply to those of others.

As consumers of the printed word, librarians rightly question the purpose behind a book or periodical. It is not always evident that they have asked the same question of the material they themselves produce. Public relations publications should have a purpose.

They also need an audience if they are to be effective. The likely nature of the intended audience needs to be considered when deciding on the language to be used in, and the style and appearance of, a proposed publication. It is quite wrong to assume that the same piece of material will be equally effective with all sections of the library's public. Non-users and users respond to different stimuli, staff and council members each require a different approach, professionals and the lay public a different emphasis, and so on.

Library publications can be used to record a library's achievements, to inform, to promote, and to persuade. These are important tasks and it is essential that they are carried out in a professional manner. Library publications should look good. This is vital because the public's perception of a library service may well be influenced, consciously or sub-consciously, by the quality of its printed material.

Stationery

A form of printed material seen by all who use, or work in or with public libraries is stationery. Because it is such an everyday commodity, it is all too easy to overlook its public relations role. Stationery reaches those parts of a library's community that other publications do not reach. It therefore plays a particularly important role in creating the right, or wrong, image of a library and its services.

Library tickets, book labels, compliment slips, letter headings, and, above all, overdue notices help to create an impression of a library as a service organization. If the impression of the service is drab and austere or old-fashioned, people will tend to think of the service as drab, austere, or old-fashioned.

If care is taken over the design and production of these everyday items, they can be instrumental in promoting a positive image of the library. It is worth taking professional advice on the use of colour and the choice of typeface. Tradition has a place, but you might want to think more than twice about using the Council's coat of arms on every piece of printed paper.

Make sure that your library's stationery conveys the right message about your library's role in your community. John Allison, chief display designer with Lambeth's Directorate of Development Services is of the opinion that: 'A royal borough . . . proud of its history and traditions will want an elegant style. Places like Bath and Harrogate will probably attach considerable importance to the dignity of their . . . notepaper. A place like Lambeth . . . where the

Everyday stationery can be used to increase your library's visibility.

day-to-day problems are tougher . . . can be more bold in its choice of design and image.'[1]

Here he is talking about the image of the local authority as a whole. In these days of corporate management, it is probable that library departments will have to use centrally designed stationery intended to promote the corporate identity of the authority, rather than that of any individual department. This can cause public librarians problems and it is a topic which we will return to in a later chapter.

Even in the 'corporate situation' the librarian can have some control over the language used in official documents. It is essential to keep such language human and wherever possible to eradicate 'town-hallese'. Is it really necessary to ask guarantors to 'certify' that a prospective member is 'a fit and proper person' to join the library? At least one library does!

Overdue notices can also be a very serious public relations liability. While one accepts that recalcitrant readers need to be reminded to return their books, there are different ways of doing this. As the illustration on page 23 shows, a touch of humour may not come amiss when reminding users of their responsibilities. Worst of all, perhaps, are the computer generated reminders which reduce both the client and the overdue material to a series of incomprehensible numbers.

Notices

Care should also be taken over the wording and design of library notices. While one can enjoy the joke provided by the library that solemnly informed its clients:

>THE LIBRARY WILL BE CLOSED FOR THE
>OFFICIAL OPENING

what, one wonders, is the effect on users of the ominous warning:

>'A BOOK MISPLACED IS A BOOK LOST'?

This and the surly:

>'THE LIBRARIAN IS NOT ABLE TO CHOOSE
>YOUR BOOKS FOR YOU'

A touch of humour does not come amiss when reminding readers of their responsibilities.

have both been seen by the writer on visits to library organizations.

Library notices, too, often seem to tell clients what they cannot or should not do, rather than what they can do. In considering the notices they place in their libraries, librarians should perhaps take note of the advice of the social psychologist Milton Rokeach. He, albeit in a different context, suggests we concentrate on 'the thou shalts of the Sermon on the mount' rather than the 'thou shalt nots of the ten commandments'.[2]

In fact, it is wise to avoid having too many notices in a library, though there are, of course, certain essential items of information, such as hours of opening or details of any new procedures, which have to be displayed. Library activities should also be publicized through notices and posters displayed inside and outside library buildings. A good poster on a visible site can be a very effective form of library publicity. Hertfordshire County Library, for example, has demonstrated this with a recent series of posters designed for display on railway stations, and aimed at the commuter public. One of these informed travellers 'OUR TICKETS ARE FREE'. A well-designed poster can also do much to add to the impact of a display.

Notices and posters must look professional. It is essential, for instance, that any lettering is well done. Even where a library does not employ a graphic display artist reasonable results can be achieved by using one of the instant lettering systems now on the market. There is also much to be said for involving a local art college or the like if there is one in the area. Apart from helping the visual image of the library, such contact is in itself a sound piece of community PR.

Annual reports

From everyday publications to one that appears once a year – the annual report. The basis of any annual report is the factual account of the work undertaken by an organization in the year under review. In the public library context, it is first and foremost a report to the library's political masters. As such, it can be a peg on which the skilful library manager can hang numerous arguments concerning the future well-being of the library service.

The report should also be a report to the library's community of users and non-users. Through it they can be reminded of what is provided by their rates and taxes.

Aiming an annual report at two or more different sections of the community can cause the librarian problems. Which audience should she or he primarily consider when preparing material? In the final analysis, the separate audiences are probably irreconcilable. Some library services have produced different versions of their annual report. One, a full account for the committee, written perhaps with 'political' matters uppermost in mind, and another, probably in summary form, presented in a style appropriate for consumption by a general audience.

When preparing material for either audience, the librarian has to decide what to include. Some positive decisions need also to be taken on what to leave out. The main body of the report should be the account of the year's work. It is here that the librarian can comment on any special problems or opportunities, express hopes and fears for the future, and generally survey the library service.

Sometimes, departmental heads can be invited to contribute their own reviews of specific service areas. If this is done, strong editorial control is required. Not all library staff are equally effective in the art of report-writing and while individual idiosyncrasies may be tolerated in reports for internal use, they may be a considerable public relations liability in a document intended for more general dissemination.

Statistics can also be a problem. There is some advantage in presenting them separately from the main report, so that those who are put off by figures are not dissuaded from reading the rest of the material. The financial statement should also be presented in a way that is relevant to the intended audience. In particular, in a report designed for the general public, one should make the figures relate to the ratepayer's own financial experience. A recent annual report from Cheshire Public Library, Connecticut, does this in a very simple yet very positive way. The cover declares 'Last year we saved you $1,790,291.83'. The text then compares the cost, to individuals, of separately purchasing books and services with the cost of providing facilities collectively through the public library. Each service is itemized in these terms and the report concludes: 'Mr and Mrs, Miss and Ms Cheshire, we gave you a $86.75 return on $5.38 investment. Your library is a money-saving institution'.

It is politic to include in the annual report the names of local politicians responsible for the library service. Staff can also be encouraged by including their names too, by noting examination successes, professional honours, and so forth in an appropriate place in the review. Like all publications, the annual report should include the full postal address of the library, the telephone and telex numbers.

Annual reports come in many shapes and sizes but most should include the basic material indicated above. The precise ordering and presentation of topics will depend on a number of things — not the least of which is finance. In the present economic climate, few library services will be able to afford to produce large, glossy brochures but, large or small, a report intended for public distribution should be professional in appearance. It is also worth remembering that pictures can be a great help in telling a story, so that a brief, well-illustrated report can often be more effective than a lengthy, verbose one.

When writing material for a report, it is wise to avoid the use of library jargon. What is an ordinary member of the public to make of the following example of library report writing? 'Staff in this division have concentrated on the conversion of stock and the re-registration of young members in preparation for the operation of the automated issue system.'

I have not gone out of my way to provide a particularly bad example but one that is sadly all too typical. Jargon may sometimes aid communication between professionals but it is a considerable barrier to communication with an outside audience.

Having produced a report the librarian must think about its effective distribution. It will of course go to members of the Council but it does no harm, and probably some good, to make it available to members of staff and also to other library authorities. PR with the library profession is important and copies should be sent to the Library Association and to library schools. A copy can also be usefully included with the 'further details' sent to job applicants. A report can be made more widely known in the community by sending copies, together with a news release summarizing its major points, to the local press and broadcasting organizations.

A well-produced and effectively distributed annual report can do much for a library's public relations. In addition to providing a historical record of the library service, it can also provide a platform from which to promote the service to legislators and to a wider audience. It can demonstrate to ratepayers what they are obtaining for their money, boost staff morale, and generally show the value of public library services to the world at large.

Guides

Another form of publication produced by most library authorities is the library guide. This can range in format from a simple duplicated sheet to a glossy prestige production. The basic aim of guides intended for users or potential users should be to introduce clients to the library and its services. Some may seek to describe the full range of services, while others may concentrate on a department or a special facility.

A well-produced guide should enable clients to take full advantage of the library and its resources. It can create an awareness of the service and this is important for the many users, and even more non-users, who are unaware of the full range of facilities available. The guide should also assist clients in their actual use of the library, for example by explaining the classification scheme. Intelligently distributed, a guide can also help promote increased use of the library service.

Sometimes a guide may be aimed at a particular section of the library's public, industry, for instance. Here, as always, the language and presentation of information should keep the nature of the audience in mind.

In addition to basic information, such as addresses, telephone and telex numbers, the guide should also include names of senior staff, details of opening hours and, of course, a brief description of the full range of services available at, and through, the library. A plan of the library is a useful addition if the size of the building warrants it and, if the total system has been described, a sketch map showing branch locations with details of transport routes can be of considerable use.

When describing library facilities and procedures, it is sound PR to emphasize what the library can do and, wherever possible, to present rules and regulations in a positive way. Where this is not appropriate then a light touch can help. For example, the West Virginia Library Commission introduce information about fines, overdues, and the like under the heading 'A few rules which keep this place going without spoiling your fun'.

Guides should be given to new users, but efforts should also be made to reach those people in the community who have not yet made the decision to use the library. Schools and colleges are an obvious target, while new residents can be reached through the 'Welcome waggon' type of organization which now operates in many neighbourhoods. Cooperation with the local authority's Housing Department could enable a library to distribute a guide to new council tenants. It does no harm to take complimentary copies when talking to community groups, while those guides of special interest to particular sections of the community can be distributed through the appropriate societies and organizations.

Another valuable type of guide is that intended for the new member of staff. It is important to make new staff feel welcome, and essential to provide them with information about the organization in which they are to spend their working days. Such a guide should describe general conditions of service, covering such topics as sickness, superannuation, leave entitlement and so on. The names of union and or staff association representatives can also be usefully included, together with a brief practical description of library services and departments, including the non-public sections. A list of service points and details of how to reach them should also be included.

One such guide not only gives details of bus routes and so on, but includes a note on nearby hostelries and other facilities: essential information for the new recruit on an 'eight o'clock relief'. A brief introduction to library jargon, local and universal acronyms can also help the new staff member. Details of Library Association membership should also be included. Such a guide can play a small but not insignificant part in helping to integrate the individual staff member into the library organization.

Newsletters

Staff newsletters are to be encouraged as a means of providing a continuous flow of information to library personnel. Newsletters can also be produced for the general public and are a useful way of informing people of what is going on in a library service. Because the requirements of the two groups are different, it is not wise to produce one newsletter for both staff and public. Indeed, before embarking on any newsletter it is worth considering if there is enough material available to produce the publication on a regular basis. Taking advantage of concessionary postal rates, some librarians in the United States use direct mail to distribute newsletters. A development of this is the production of special-interest direct mail newsletters. Plainedge Library has followed this policy, its Director, Joseph Eisner, believing that newsletters which provide information to selected groups are a logical outgrowth of information and referral and 'outreach' services.

Lists

Lists of library material from simple booklists to full-scale bibliographies have long been a favourite form of library publication. However, like all publications they should not be produced unless there is a sound reason for their appearance. Catalogues can be published to draw clients' attention to additions to stock over a period of time, or to reflect the holdings of a special collection as, for example, with catalogues of play-sets. Booklists can introduce clients to items they have missed; they can show potential clients the library's holdings in their special interest field; or help bring together material on a topic which is dispersed by the classification scheme and/or the arrangement of the library. For example, a list on 'growing up' would need to draw together subjects from many parts of the Dewey decimal classification scheme. Other lists might be issued in conjunction with a display or exhibition.

Lists are useful for staff as well as library users but their PR value is severely negated if a library does not have the resources to meet the demand created by a list. The same is true of any other promotional activity.

Local studies

Local studies collections have always been a source for booklists and catalogues, but in the past few years some libraries have adopted a much more positive approach in promoting local studies material. In some areas, local studies publications are now a minor industry, providing a useful source of income and creating community interest in collections sometimes considered too esoteric for the general public.

A number of libraries have published full-scale books reviewing the history of an area. Lambeth, for example, has published well-researched works on Clapham and West Norwood.[3]/[4] Other libraries have used material kept in collections as a basis for publication. *Old Philadelphia,*[5] for example, is based on a collection of photographs and prints held by the Free Library of Philadelphia. Lambeth's music hall 'jackdaw'[6] is a collection of documents reproduced from originals held in the Minet Library. Postcards can now be found for sale in a great many libraries, as can local studies leaflets on individuals, institutions, and places of local significance. The London Borough of Sutton has produced some decorative maps of local areas, some of which are hand-coloured. Sales would suggest that these now adorn many a suburban home.

Considerations

Conceiving, writing, and producing library publications can be an exciting process. However, it is little use preparing publications that are not going to be read because they are, or look, uninteresting. Neither should one become so carried away that a planned publication costs too much to produce at all. In dealing with some of the different types of publication, we have already indicated some specific practical considerations. In this section we turn to some general matters which need to be considered by librarians contemplating any kind of printed publication.

Cost

In this day and age, the first of these considerations has to be cost. A look at the economics of library publications must include some discussion of such matters as the reprographic process to be used, staff time involved in preparing and collating copy, and the costs of distribution. Added together, the real costs of even a simple publication can be quite significant. Costs can be offset by making a charge for a publication and/or by carrying advertising, for example from a local bookseller.

Production

Those members of staff closely involved in the production of a publication should have some basic knowledge of reprography and also be familiar enough with copy preparation to be able to instruct printers in a way they will understand. The relationship with a printer is an important one and the library's choice of printer can make or mar the final product. When the librarian has to follow local government tendering procedures, his or her choice of printer may be restricted, but if a quality job is required the librarian should attempt to persuade council members that the cheapest is not always the best. This is especially true if specialist work is required, for example, the faithful reproduction of original local study prints.

A good printer is not only one who produces work of quality but one who will also give clients a production schedule and who will in fact deliver on the agreed date. If possible, it is worth visiting the printing works. The librarian, or the member of staff with specialist responsibilities for publications, will profit if he or she builds up a good working relationship with the printing firm.

Design

Graphic design is more fully dealt with in a later chapter but decisions do have to be taken about such things as the choice of paper and typeface. Where a publication has a cover, some consideration should be given to its design. Any publication has to compete for attention and a cover should be designed so as to encourage the potential user to look at the material inside. When an illustration is used on the cover, or indeed anywhere else in a publication, care should be taken to clear any copyright considerations.

Language

As we have already emphasized, thought should be given to the use of language. Jargon should be avoided. As a general rule, the written word in library publications should be brief, simple, and clear. People do not want to have to read through something several times before they are able to understand what it means. Where appropriate, the language of any minority group in the community should be used, which may mean producing two or more versions of general publications. Where a specific group is aimed at, then obviously the language of the group should be used, likewise a leaflet promoting services for the partially sighted should be produced in a suitably large type.

There is much to be said for developing a house style so that all publications emanating from a particularly library service use the same form of spelling and the same presentation of figures, headings, acronyms, and trade names.

Frequency

The frequency with which a publication is produced will vary with circumstances and the only general rule is that they should appear so as to meet the requirements of their intended audience. It is important that regular publications, such as lists of additions, do in fact appear regularly so that users begin to expect them at a

The appropriate language. New York Public Library's Chatham Square Branch has a large Chinese language book collection. Many of the staff speak both English and Chinese. The publicity reflects the library's multicultural interests.

particular time. It is best not to commit a library to a regular series if the regularity is likely to suffer through lack of staff or other resources.

Distribution

Decisions need also to be taken as to how many copies to produce. This will depend in part on the economics of the production method chosen. Where there are a known number of recipients the decision is comparatively easy but where this is not the case some careful market research is required. Of course, in an ideal world a library would not embark on the production of a publication without some idea of the size of the potential audience, but . . .

In order to reach that audience publications have to be distributed. Where mailing lists are used for this, it is essential that they are kept up-to-date. If the publication is one of some substance it is important to have it listed in the appropriate bibliographies. In addition, review copies should be sent to suitable newspapers and journals. It is also to be hoped that librarians will not forget their responsibilities, as publishers, to the copyright libraries.

Ideas

There are many variations on the basic theme of library publications. The discussion of publications that use media other than paper and print is left for later chapters. When considering a publications programme involving some of the things discussed above, the librarian can do no better than to seek out good and bad examples of the kind of material he or she wishes to produce. The search for such items should not be restricted to the library world. Many business and commercial organizations produce high quality PR material which is often available for the asking. Such material often contains visual and verbal ideas which can be adapted for use in the library context.

Advertisements abound in all kinds of publications and a librarian entrusted with the PR function should maintain an 'ideas

Commercial ideas can be adapted for use in the library context.

file' culled from newspapers, magazines, and other sources. Material produced by other libraries can provide a guide as to what — or in some cases what not — to do, and this should be collected whenever the opportunity arises. There are a number of 'how to do library PR good/cheap' books on the market, and though they are mainly American, they can be obtained through the Library Association's library. Some titles are listed in the bibliography. The Library Association also maintains files of annual reports and other publicity material. The American Library Association keeps a complete set of PR scrapbooks submitted for the John Cotton Dana Library Public Relations Awards. Some libraries now market publications packs. For example, the City of Coventry issues a *Stationery Handbook* and a *Stationery/Publicity Kit* as part of its 'Aids to Library Education' series. Any library which produces a variety of publications should put together a sample publicity pack to give to visitors, new council members, and the like.

Library publications have been called the 'sales literature of the library'. As we have indicated above, they can be that and more. They are an integral part of any library's public relations programme. For even today when, as we show in later chapters, other promotional outlets are available, the printed word remains an important medium of communication for use within and without a library organization.

REFERENCES

1 Quoted in Freeman, L and Cossey, C 'Creating the right image', *Municipal and Public Services Journal,* 7 December 1973.
2 Rokeach, M 'Faith, hope, bigotry', *Psychology Today* 3 (11), 1970.
3 Smith, E F *Clapham,* London Borough of Lambeth, 1976.
4 Wilson, J B *The story of Norwood* (prepared by H A Wilson), London Borough of Lambeth, 1973.
5 Looney, R F *Old Philadelphia in early photographs 1839–1914,* Dover Publications in cooperation with the Free Library of Philadelphia, 1976.
6 O'Rourke, E (*comp.*) *Lambeth Music Hall,* London Borough of Lambeth, 1977.

Chapter 4
Audio-Visual Public Relations

Paper and print is not the only publication method available to librarians. Just as the stock of public libraries now increasingly includes audio-visual publications, so libraries use audio-visual methods to promote their services. These methods can include gramophone records, video, film and tape-slide presentations.

'A tape-slide presentation consists of a sequence of projected slide transparencies synchronized with a tape-recorded sound track, which may consist of a verbal commentary, music or sound effects, or a combination of any of these elements.'[1] Tape-slide productions can be used to convey factual information about a library service, to instruct users (a common use in academic libraries), to promote the service, and to stimulate potential clients to join. Presentations can range from simple single-projector shows to sophisticated multiscreen productions. An example of the latter is the West Virginia Library Commission's recent presentation to the Governor's Conference on public libraries. This utilized seven projectors, three screens, and around one thousand images.

Tape-slide shows can be mounted for group viewing or for casual viewing by visitors to a library stand at an exhibition or as a display in a library foyer. A tape-slide presentation can be a very effective means of communication but much depends on the thought and skill that goes into its production and preparation.

Preparing a script

When preparing a script it is important to keep the intended audience in mind and to adopt a form and style appropriate to their needs. Before actually writing the script it is helpful to make a note of the main topics that are to be covered. A common mistake is to try and include too much information, for there is a limit to what any audience can remember. (As a simple test of this try and list how many items you can recall from last night's main television news.)

When writing the final script it is necessary to be quite ruthless in discarding statistics, facts, and ideas. Only those which help achieve the aim of your presentation should be retained. The information that is presented must be accurate and should be arranged in a logical sequence. The opening sequence is most important for it is through this that an audience's attention is lost or engaged. A story-line can sometimes be helpful in holding the audience's interest throughout the length of a presentation.

In scriptwriting all the usual rules apply. Sentences should be kept short — around 10 to 20 words — and the words used should be easy to understand; jargon of course, is to be avoided. An informal style is often ideal so do not be afraid to make the script human, including the use of 'we', 'I' and 'you' if appropriate. If a known presenter is to read the script, his or her own style should be kept in mind. One interesting audio presentation by a British public library failed completely because the scriptwriter made no effort to capture the style of the well-known disc jockey engaged to present the material.

Professional broadcasters should not need to be told to vary the pace of their delivery and their tone of voice, but others making a recording should be reminded of these simple techniques. When actually taping the piece, one should make sure that the recording is carried out under reasonable conditions. An audience will not be impressed by sounds of passing traffic, the rustle of a script, or voices off. If possible the recording should be made in a studio. Few, if any, British public libraries possess this kind of facility but you may well find that your local radio station will be willing to help out.

Music can often be a useful addition to the spoken commentary. It is important to choose music that is sympathetic to the mood of the presentation. One must also avoid the temptation to use 'grand' music. If the introductory soundtrack leads the audience to expect a production of *Ben Hur* or *Star Wars* proportions, a modest programme, however well made and produced, will come as something of an anti-climax.

Remember too that commercial recordings are covered by copyright and be sure to check that all copyright requirements have been met before making a recording. Local musicians can provide an alternative to a commercial recording, provided a check is first made on their reputation. A presentation can be spoilt by a less-than-professional musical performance.

Slides

The slide part of a tape-slide presentation needs to be prepared just as thoroughly. Any old slide will not do. Pictures, for instance, must fit the shape of the screen. This means using horizontal pictures. Unmasked vertical pictures will stray off the edge of the screen. Like the written script, the visual information should be presented in an uncomplicated manner. The sequence of slides should be logical and care should be taken to ensure a visual continuity from image to image. Pictures should not be kept on the screen for too long: experts recommend five seconds per slide, although if the audience is being asked to assimilate a relatively complicated idea or image, this time can be doubled. At the other end of the time-scale some pictures can be flicked quickly on and off the screen for a subliminal effect.

It is necessary to exercise strict quality control in selecting pictures for the programme. Over-exposed or out-of-focus slides must be rejected, as should those in which any important text is not legible.

The success of a tape-slide programme depends very much on obtaining the correct match between aural and visual information. When preparing the presentation, the pictures, the words, and the music should be considered together and matched so as to produce a whole which will effectively convey the library's message.

Tape-slide checklist

In a recent dissertation submitted to the University of Sheffield, Cherie Neale included a useful checklist for anybody contemplating the production of tape-slide presentation. This is reproduced below.

Planning the script:
1. List at the beginning the main topics to be covered
2. Arrange them in a logical and acceptable order
3. Start with a familiar or simple concept
4. Identify each step as it occurs
5. Present each step separately
6. If possible give your presentation a story-line

Writing the script:
7. Use plain words
8. Avoid jargon
9. Use simple sentence constructions
10. Use short sentences
11. Use shortened forms
12. Avoid an impersonal, formal style of writing
13. Listen to the sound of the words
14. Write for talking
15. Talk while you write
16. Write linking sentences
17. Do not overload your script with detail
18. Do not include irrelevant material for the sake of accuracy
19. Group like topics together
20. Avoid distracting statements
21. Avoid ambiguities in the writing
22. Keep the presentation shorter than 20 minutes
23. Write in a style which suits the presenter

Speaking the commentary:
24. Vary pace, emphasis, and inflection
25. Let your personality emerge
26. Do not worry about the technicalities of production
27. Concentrate on the sense of the words
28. Do not worry how you sound

Photographing text:
- 29 Choose an example without a distracting feature
- 30 Choose a typical example
- 31 Ensure the text is legible if the viewer is meant to read it
- 32 Frame your picture to eliminate unwanted material
- 33 Do not split your viewer's focus of attention

Photographing books:
- 34 Use composition to focus attention
- 35 Use composition to affect attitudes
- 36 Use composition, colour, lighting to show books to best advantage

In general:
- 37 Remember, the viewer reads from left to right and from top to bottom
- 38 Do not in general read out verbatim a verbal statement on the screen
- 39 When justified, read out items in the order in which they occur
- 40 Ensure continuity between adjacent slides
- 41 Do not let a slide outstay its welcome
- 42 Do not remove it too quickly
- 43 Change the slide at the right point in the commentary
- 44 Fulfil the viewer's expectations
- 45 Remember that consistency of style will give coherence to your presentation
- 46 Do not mix techniques unnecessarily
- 47 Avoid overloading a slide with visual information
- 48 Remember that the projected image of black on white is very bright
- 49 Always decide on slides and commentary in conjunction
- 50 Use any technique for some purpose, not just to make a change

As Ms Neale points out, these are not rules but simply suggestions and there may be times when something different is done for effect. However, for most PR purposes they are suggestions that are well worth following.

Presenting a programme

However good, a production can be ruined by poor presentation. It is therefore essential to take certain precautions before presenting a programme. Before giving a show you should make sure that all the equipment is in good working order. In addition to the obvious precaution of having a spare lamp available, you should check the electricity supply and the quality of the blackout. If the show is being taken to an outside hall, it is particularly important to check ahead on the last two points. Even today, 13-amp power points are not universal! If time permits it is always wise to run through a programme privately before any public showing.

There is really nothing too difficult about presenting a tape-slide show. There is a range of strong and simply operated equipment on the market and with practice most library staff should be able to use 'the big picture show' with some effect. For those who need help, the Council for Educational Technology issues a series of very simple booklets on operating tape-slide equipment. These deal with basic things, such as 'organizing the slides' and 'inserting the slide' and are worth reading. Details are given at the end of the chapter.[2]

Films and filming

From a big picture show to a moving picture show. Film is a potent medium of communication and is widely used in commercial public relations work. However, it is also an expensive medium and only a few public libraries have embarked on film-making.

Writing in 1973, K.C. Harrison[3] said, "There is a crying need for an outstanding library film". That is probably still true today, though Sheffield Public Library may have a possible contender in their recently released *Books and Beyond*. Sheffield is in fact one of a small number of British public libraries to have already produced a film. Its earlier effort, *Books in Hand,* made in 1955, if not outstanding, was certainly worthwhile. The new film is a 16mm colour production which runs for approximately 29 minutes. It shows the use made of the City Libraries by a typical Sheffield family and its primary purpose is to demonstrate the range of facilities available from and through the library service. It cost about £10,000 to make.

In addition to being a valuable promotional tool a film can also be a useful aid to staff training and recruitment and, especially in the American context, fund raising activities. It can also be used at the international level and in fact the British Council partly subsidized the Sheffield production and intends to use it in its own international activities.

A film, then, is likely to cost in the region of £10,000. What can one expect to receive for this kind of money? Working within this figure Sheffield obtained three weeks shooting time and employed the services of a local film production company, television actors and an award winning director. The library also took professional advice on the script. Such costs may be partly recouped by selling the final production and/or by hiring it out to interested organizations. From a sales point of view it is wise to make copies available in both film and a video format.

What audience?

The Sheffield film is intended for a general audience but a film aimed at a small but influential audience can also be a worthwhile endeavour. This was certainly the case with a film produced by the New York Public Library with the objective of raising funds from the city's business community. It shows the departments and services of the NYPL, emphasizing their particular relevance to the business and commercial world.

This film not only looks at departments with obvious commercial connections but also, for instance, at the Oriental Collection. Here, the businessman is reminded that this department can help him with all kinds of information, ranging from general facts about the economy of the Orient to a telephone number found through the Tokyo 'phone book. Throughout the film the professional presenter constantly reminds the audience that the New York Public Library provides a valuable service: 'You may not be aware how much you use it but you use it.' He then stresses the financial problems facing the library and, by using the example of previous

44   *The Visible Library*

business benefactors, encourages the business audience to support the library. This production has been shown to business and commercial organizations with considerable success.

Planning a film

Whether a production is intended for a general or a specialized audience, certain factors have to be considered by a librarian contemplating the use of film. First, he or she must ask the following questions. What are the objectives of the film? Could these objectives be as satisfactorily met by other means? For what audience is the film intended? And, of course, how much will it cost? If these questions produce satisfactory answers, the librarian must begin to think about engaging the professional help that it is essential to use. This should include technical staff, actors, a producer, and a director. Before finally choosing a director or production company, the librarian should try to see examples of their work and attempt to obtain some objective assessment of their professional reputation.

When planning the film it is worth bearing in mind the fact that a film is something that the library will want to use for a number of years. Thus, in a rapidly changing library world one should avoid describing the latest piece of equipment as 'new', because it will not be in a few years time when the film is still being shown. So treat the new on-line service or whatever as routine. Similarly, if hanges are about to take place, but are not yet in operation, it is quite in order to simulate the future.

Distribution

Once a film has been completed it is important to ensure that it achieves maximum distribution and sales. Copies should be deposited with film libraries, such as that run by the Central Office of Information. Details of the production should be included in film catalogues. Information about the film should also be sent to professional journals, library schools, professional associations, and other bodies likely to be interested.

The film can be shown when members of staff are invited to talk to organizations. Women's Institutes, Rotary Clubs, and the like provide a library with a ready-made audience for a film though, in most cases, the library will have to supply the projection equipment and an operator. It is also useful to arrange special showings for invited audiences, including the local press and radio. Other opportunities to show the film will come up from time to time at exhibitions, county shows, fairs, conferences, and so forth. The precautions to be taken before a public showing of a tape-slide programme, indicated above, also of course apply to a film presentation.

It is not intended that the information provided here should be sufficiently detailed to enable a librarian to produce a film. Filmmaking is a job for professionals. If a library authority cannot afford to employ professional help and advice it should not embark on film production. A second-rate film is simply not worth making.

In some circumstances, a film strip may be the answer for a library operating on a limited budget. Specialist companies operating in this field are capable of producing quite sophisticated programmes which are literally light years away from the old magic lantern image.

Discs

Audio, in the form of gramophone records, has been used to promote public library services. Annual reports and library guides have been produced in the flexidisc format. The flexidisc is widely used by industry and commercial concerns — anyone who has found himself on a *Readers Digest* mailing list is almost certain to have received one. They are not too expensive to produce. At 1980 prices, the unit pressing charge ranges from 16.5p to 2.75p per 7 inch disc, the exact price depending on the length of the run, the thickness of the vinyl used, and whether the disc is single or double-sided. There are a number of variations on the basic theme of the black single-sided disc. For instance, it is possible to produce a publication in which the playing surface of the disc forms part of a text or illustration.

The London Borough of Sutton used a flexi-disc to promote children's services at its new Central Library.

NOTES AND REFERENCES

1 Neale, C A 'The use of tape-slide in library instruction', a study submitted in partial fulfilment of the requirements for the degree of Master of Arts in Librarianship at the University of Sheffield, 1977, (unpublished).
2 The Council for Educational Technology is situated at 3 Devonshire Street, London W1N 2BA. The following titles are recommended: *Operating a cassette tape recorder, Operating a film strip projector, Operating a slide projector, Operating a tape-slide programme.* All four were printed and produced by PETRAS, Newcastle upon Tyne Polytechnic 1976.
3 Harrison, K C *Public relations for librarians,* Deutsch, 1973.

Chapter 5
Design and Display

Graphic design is work for a skilled person. The talents and skills required in a professional librarian are not the same as those required by a professional graphic display artist. Librarians or library assistants who are 'good with their hands' are only rarely, if at all, going to produce material of professional quality. The aim of this section is, not to enable librarians to become artists, but to provide them with some practical insight into the needs and problems of artists employed by library authorities. Such insight should help both parties develop a productive working relationship.

Many library organizations do now employ professional graphic artists on a full-time basis. Other libraries employ professional artists from time to time. The working relationship between the librarian and the artist will be enhanced if the librarian cares enough about good graphic design to be able to recognize it at least.

Carol Bryan,[1] to whom the writer owes many of the thoughts in the first part of this chapter, says that recognizing good graphic design 'requires well-developed taste, selection abilities, and confident judgement'.[2] Such skills should not be uncommon among librarians, though they may lack the 'sound knowledge of design talent, technical skill (and) execution' required by the artist.

Briefing the designer

The librarian who cares about the image of the library needs to be concerned with the quality of graphic design, because the visual information given via a library's publications, notices, displays, and guiding contributes to the public's perception of the library and the services it offers. The librarian may well have ideas about the image and/or the service that he or she wishes to promote but it is the job of an artist to translate those ideas into a visual form. In order to be able to do this the artist will need detailed information from the library staff regarding the purpose and form of the work required. The artist should be told the primary aim of the publication, be it to inform, promote or instruct. He or she will also need to know the nature of the audience for whom the work is primarily needed. Such factors will affect an artist's treatment of any particular theme.

The designer will also require the following practical information:

1 The number of copies required
2 Any limitations on size
3 The date by which the work is to be delivered.

On the last point, do try to give your artist time for creative thinking; the final result will be all the better for it. In most large library systems it is worth producing a Job Order form, designed so as to give the artist the type of information indicated in this paragraph and above. Such a formalized version of a job requirement should not, of course, take the place of regular consultation between the librarian and the artist over questions of copy and design. In many cases, a librarian may wish to see several rough drafts of a design before the final product is agreed.

Getting the message across

A library's visual communications, like its verbal ones, should be easy to follow. Complicated layouts are best avoided. It is advisable for publications to have just one point of major visual interest. The relationship between the text and the design is crucial, they should work together to convey the desired message. The artwork should reinforce — at times exaggerate — the point that is being made by the words.

Although we have throughout emphasized the need for a professional approach to library artwork, there is one exception to this general rule. If a library promotes craft activities or the like within its children's services, these can often be the source of valuable material. There are occasions when, given the right circumstances, children's art can be incorporated into a publication or display. Artists sometimes spend a lifetime trying to recapture the artistic world of their childhood and at times the real thing can be very effective. Indeed, The Library Association recognized this when the cover design for its publication on service to ethnic minorities[3] was based on a drawing made by a six-year-old boy. This, however, is very much the exception that proves the rule that it pays to employ a professional.

Guiding

Good graphic design should be present in all the material produced by a library organization. This especially includes the often neglected area of guiding. Compared to that found in large stores, airports, or even railway stations, library guiding often leaves much to be desired. Yet good guiding is essential because it is through guiding that clients are made aware of the services available, where to find them, and how to use them.

For example, directional signs should be clear, with large lettering and a consistent colour scheme.

The aim of such guiding should be to make the library building and its facilities and services easy to use. This involves not only the production of directional and shelf signs, but also aids on how to use the catalogue and general information about services. In areas where a significant number of clients or potential clients have a first language other than English, that language should also appear on library signposts and notices.

Library guiding is in fact a subject in itself, and it has been covered elsewhere,[4] but for PR purposes suffice it to say that poorly produced guiding projects a very poor image of the public library as a service institution. All too often, the writer has seen new well-designed and pleasant library buildings spoilt by poor and/or inadequate guiding — including the unforgivable, handwritten shelf guides attached to stack ends with adhesive tape. In larger library buildings, it is worthwhile displaying a floor plan to enable clients to find their way from one department to another.

The library guiding reflects the language of the community who use this branch of the Brooklyn Library. (*Photo: Author*)

Display

The air of amateurism sometimes seen in guiding and the design of publications also pervades library display activities, thus negating their effect. Displays can play a significant part in a library's public relations activities. They can be used to bring clients' attention to various topics and materials, to exploit and increase the use of the library's stock, to inform, to bring together material that may be separated by a classification scheme, and to improve the general atmosphere of the library. A well-mounted and strategically sited display can, for instance, do much to brighten a dull library foyer.

Like all PR activities, displays need planning. A programme should be worked out well in advance of displays being mounted. In a large public library system, displays could and should circulate from area to area. In preparing a programme, it is wise to incorporate a degree of flexibility so that displays on topical matters of local and national interest can be mounted if the opportunity presents itself.

Ideas for display are only limited by the imagination and initiative of the library staff concerned, but a useful source of inspiration can be the *Wilson Library Bulletin* which for many years has carried a regular feature on library display.

Types of display

Displays can also help a library further its contacts with the local community. Local organizations should be encouraged to display material in the library. Not only will this introduce users to new ideas, but it can attract non-users who have an interest in the activities of the organization concerned. Collectors, who are to be found in most communities, can be a valuable source of display material and themes. This is particularly true of those who have collected artefacts of local significance. Recently, one or two library committees have turned down, on political or moral grounds, requests from organizations to mount displays on contemporary issues. This is a pity because the public library is surely the right place for the community to exchange legitimate views and ideas.

Mounting a display

There is a wide range of easily erected display equipment on the market which makes it possible for staff who have the appropriate skills, and who are given the necessary professional help with graphics, to mount satisfactory displays. If, as is sometimes the case, display work is made the responsibility of a talented junior, then he or she should be allowed adequate time in which to do the work. The library management of course has the responsibility to ensure that such time is well used. After all, for most juniors display work will come as a welcome relief from some of the more mundane routine duties.

A library display can very often be enlivened by the use of a 'non library' object. Most clients expect to find books in libraries, but the addition of something completely different to a book display may make them look more than twice at an exhibit. There is really no limit to the type of object that can be used in this way. The London Borough of Islington recently used a police motorcycle to draw attention to '150 years of police work'. Less dramatically but equally effectively, libraries have used sets of gardening tools to enhance displays of gardening books, and pieces of electronic equipment in displays drawing attention to science-fiction titles.

Objects of this kind can often be borrowed from local firms and organizations for the 'price' of an acknowledgement. However, when borrowing a costly item it is essential to ensure that the library has adequate insurance cover. Accidents can and do happen, even in the best regulated libraries. Where the material on display needs protection from dust or constant handling, it is worth investing in a set of moulded acrylic covers designed to fit over standard display screens.

Display equipment is constantly being developed by the various manufacturers operating in the field, and the member of staff responsible for graphics and display work should keep in touch with these new developments. This is easily achieved by putting the library on manufacturers' mailing lists and by visiting appropriate exhibitions. Even if the library never buys a piece of equipment, the catalogues in themselves contain a wealth of ideas.

Displaying books

Even though a good library display will make use of pictures, photographs, arts objects and other artefacts, books still often form the basis of such efforts. Where this is the case, it is useful to issue a booklist in conjunction with the display. If the stock can stand it — and one should think twice about mounting a display if it cannot — clients should be allowed, indeed encouraged, to borrow from a display of books. Behavioural scientists who have studied shoppers in supermarkets have observed that people are often reluctant to break the symmetry of a display. It is possible, therefore, that books are more likely to be taken from a display that has an informal appearance.

While on the subject of books, it is strange how many librarians fail to realize that book jackets are designed for full frontal display. A great amount of time, skill, and money goes into the production and design of jackets and this is often wasted by traditional library shelving methods. A few sloping shelves, allowing books to be displayed with their jackets facing the potential reader, would encourage use and also help overcome the sometimes rather dull appearance of long rows of shelving. A novel idea, seen by the writer on a visit to Poland, is to have brief biographies of authors, with portraits, displayed in appropriate parts of the fiction sequence. There is, in fact, a close relationship between stock exploitation and many aspects of public relations. Stores, supermarkets, and other commercial organizations realized long ago that there is a causal relationship between the physical presentation of their goods and their sales figures.

Even a well-presented display loses impact if it is allowed to remain for too long. After a while, even the best display can become just part of the library scenery. Displays should therefore be changed frequently.

Displays in other places

Although we have so far written about displays as part of the library environment, there is absolutely no reason why library displays have to be restricted to library buildings. Indeed, if the object of a display is to attract new clients, it should, almost by definition, be mounted on premises other than a library: clinics, banks, swimming pools, stations, cinema foyers, and many other places where people gather, are all suitable sites for professionally mounted library displays. Such sites can be used for general promotion purposes but it can also be effective to link the library display with the use made of the building concerned. Hence, 'Films and filming' or 'The book of the film' could be ideal topics for exhibits mounted in cinemas or at local film societies.

It is perhaps unlikely that the local record store would wish to carry a display advertising a free library record service but, such difficulties apart, local shops and organizations are very often willing to cooperate with libraries on this kind of project. Of course, it can and should be argued that a well-mounted display could help their trade as well!

Exhibitions

It is a moot point just when a display becomes an exhibition but, with the increasing popularity of county shows, town fairs, career conventions, and similar activities, there are now many opportunities for public libraries to exhibit their wares. At such events, a professional approach is perhaps even more important. A library service participating in one of these functions will, more often than not, be in direct competition with organizations that have far greater resources set aside for promotional activities. I recall with some pleasure taking part in a careers convention where the library stand held its own, despite being sandwiched between a gun turret promoting the army and a police car advertising careers in the police force. This was achieved by means of a professionally mounted exhibition and the use of photographs, and (at that time) lesser-known library stock items, such as long-playing records.

At an outside show a mobile library van can form the basis of an attractive exhibit. The best exhibition stands display three-dimensional objects and, where appropriate, are backed up by pictures and diagrams. Recorded sound, if permitted by the organizers, and visual aids can also give a stand that all-important 'extra' appeal. The self-contained sound/slide projectors that are currently on the market are most useful for this form of presentation.

It is essential to have on the stand staff who can deal confidently and effectively with enquiries about the library and its services. Those enquiries that cannot be satisfied at the time should be followed up as soon as possible. At the risk of offending feminists, it has to be said that professional public relations practitioners advise that 'if female staff are employed they should be chosen for their looks and personality as well as for their intelligence or linguistic ability'.[5]

The costs of taking part in an outside exhibition can be considerable. At some commercial shows the site will have to be paid for. In addition, there will be charges for transport and insurance, while staffing a stand may involve the payment of overtime and/or accommodation costs.

At times, independent exhibitions can be mounted by and in a library. In such cases, it is the responsibility of the library staff to organize and publicize the total event. This may involve arranging an opening ceremony and providing facilities for the local press and broadcasting organizations. The press should receive invitations in good time and a member of staff should be deputed to look after their needs on the day of the event. Unless it is a really major exhibition, it will normally be opened by the appropriate chairperson. This will gain the library some publicity, but an exhibition can become a springboard for much additional publicity if a radio, television, or sports personality can be persuaded to perform the opening ceremony.

In the same way that a library should keep a file of its publications, it should also maintain a record of its participation in exhibitions. Library displays and exhibition stands should always be photographed for the PR record.

NOTES AND REFERENCES

1   Formerly with the Exposure Division of the West Virginia Library Commission, Carol Bryan now runs her own graphic design and copywriting busi-

ness. This is known as Carol Bryan Imagines and operates out of 100 Byus Drive, Charleston, West Virginia, 25311, USA. Ms Bryan is also the publisher of *The Library Imagination Paper!*: a graphic design 'how to' which also includes 'ready-to-go art and copy'.
2 Bryan, C 'Graphics' in Moran, I (comp.) *The library public relations recipe book*, Public Relations Section, Library Administration Division, American Library Association, 1978.
3 Clough, E A & Quarmby, J *A public library service for ethnic minorities in Great Britain,* Library Association, 1978.
4 See, for example: Carey, R J P *Library guiding,* Bingley, 1974.
5 Black, S *Practical public relations* 3rd ed., Pitman, 1970.

Chapter 6
Press Relations

Even today, when other media are available, many PR professionals regard press relations as 'the most important single part of public relations'.[1] Press relations for a public library, perhaps more than for any other kind of organization, should be a two-way process. It will certainly do a library's PR endeavours no harm if journalists come to regard it as a source of accurate information for use in their own day-to-day work. Reporters working on feature stories frequently require background material and the library is often the ideal agency to provide it. The more journalists come to think of the public library as a reliable source of information, the more likely they are to use a story that the library itself initiates.

Is your correction really necessary?

At times, journalists will take an interest in a library in a way that a librarian may not entirely welcome. Local papers in particular tend to promote themselves as protectors of the public purse and, as public sector institutions, libraries sometimes come under close scrutiny. In the same way, poor standards of service or ungracious public servants will, quite rightly, receive attention. We have to admit that at times such critical attention is justified but there will also be times when journalists, being human, get something wrong. When that happens the librarian should think more than twice before demanding a correction. If the matter is important enough and/or the error gross enough, by all means have it corrected but first consider if a correction is really necessary.

If a library's reputation is good in the first place it should be able to overcome the occasional misrepresentation. It is better for all concerned if there is a degree of cooperation between the local librarian and the local press, although it would be a very foolish librarian who would expect such cooperation to interfere with the traditional and greatly valued press freedom and independence. No reputable or responsible journalist will want to be in the pocket of a librarian or for that matter any other local government officer.

This does not mean that personal contact between the librarian and the local press is not desirable; on the contrary, it can be very productive. By getting to know local editors and their reporters, librarians can provide themselves with many valuable opportunities to advance the cause of their service. The journalist's trade depends on a continuous supply of information and ideas, and editors and reporters are always ready to listen to constructive and newsworthy suggestions.

The local press, in particular, can play a part in developing a library's community relations, while specialist groups and interests can be reached through the publications serving their particular needs. Librarians should not forget the specialist needs of their colleagues and the professional and local government press should also be kept informed of library news and developments.

Press releases

The news release is the basis of press relations. Editors receive many such releases every day of their working lives and a library press release will compete for editorial space with those from many other organizations. A newsworthy story will always be welcomed by the press and, all other things being equal, it is the way that the information is presented in a release that will influence an editor's decision to use, or not to use, it. To be realistic, only very rarely will a library story be of such importance or impact that an editor feels it must be included at all costs.

A news release should, therefore, be presented in such a way as to help an editor assess quickly the value of the piece for a paper's readers. A newspaper editor wants facts — he or she does not want to wade through a vast quantity of turgid prose, over-written by a librarian seeking to emulate the novelists that grace — or disgrace — library shelves. The following is only a slightly exaggerated example of this genre.

> **NEWS FROM BIBLIOVILLE PUBLIC LIBRARY**
> Stenton Road, Biblioville, BV2 1AX, Tel. 1290
>
> *Chief Librarian thanks Old Stager*
>
> The snow was thick on the ground in Stenton, Biblioville when 66-year-old Ted Lister left his home on Monday morning. For Ted it was another routine day as he made his way to the station to catch the little pay train that wound its way through the picturesque Stenton countryside to Biblioville.
>
> It was not until he reached the library where he worked as a caretaker that Ted found out that this was not to be just another day. In fact it was to be a very special day indeed!
>
> 'A day for marking the career of a model local authority employee' was how Chief Librarian Thomas Jenner described it when he presented Ted with a cheque for £50 in honour of 'a lifetime of devoted service'. Addressing Ted's library colleagues, Mr Jenner said that Mr Lister had joined the Biblioville Council service in 1929 and over the years he had 'seen many and varied changes in library buildings'.
>
> With a voice full of emotion, 'the library's oldest stager' thanked his friends and colleagues for their gift and recalled the days of his first chief librarian, Edward Latham, a stern chief who would inspect the quality of the polishing on the library counter each morning.
>
> The new Biblioville Public Library was opened by the Lord Lieutenant of the County in 1975. With its bright, inviting decor and computerized procedures it is recognized as one of the finest libraries in the United Kingdom.

Structure

When writing a press release it is essential to be economical with words. A good release will answer those vital questions: Who? What? Why? When? Where? If possible, this should be accomplished in the first paragraph. Further information relevant to the story should then be presented in order of importance. This order may vary according to the intended audience. Any background material should be included in the last paragraph. A quick look at the stories published in newspapers will confirm that most use this 'inverted pyramid' structure. It is a form of presentation that should be followed when writing library press releases, because it enables an editor to cut a story to fit the space available without it losing its point. For the same reason, each paragraph should be self-contained so that a single one can be cut out if necessary.

Presentation

There are certain conventions regarding news releases that journalists expect and the librarian issuing a release should abide by them. First, a release should be presented on headed paper. Most libraries send out enough releases to make the production of special news-release stationery worthwhile. Some examples are shown on page 61. The date of the release should be clear, as should any time embargo. An embargo will not be necessary for most library purposes and in the majority of cases the release should be marked 'IMMEDIATE'. Nearly always, a newspaper will provide its own headline for a story but it can do no harm to provide your own — providing it is short and unambiguous.

The visual presentation of the information is important. A news release should be clearly typed, using double spacing, on one side of the paper only. Wide margins (about $1\frac{1}{2}$ inches) should be left at the edge of the paper and extra space between paragraphs to enable an editor to mark the copy and write cross-heads. It can be misleading to underline words because for printers this is an instruction to set the words in italics.

Most releases should be no longer than about 250 words which means they can usually be accommodated on one side of a sheet of A4 paper. If, as sometimes happens, the release needs a second or third sheet then 'more', or some other appropriate indication, should be written at the bottom of the sheet. Paragraphs should not be broken between sheets. At the end of the release indicate the fact by the word 'ends'.

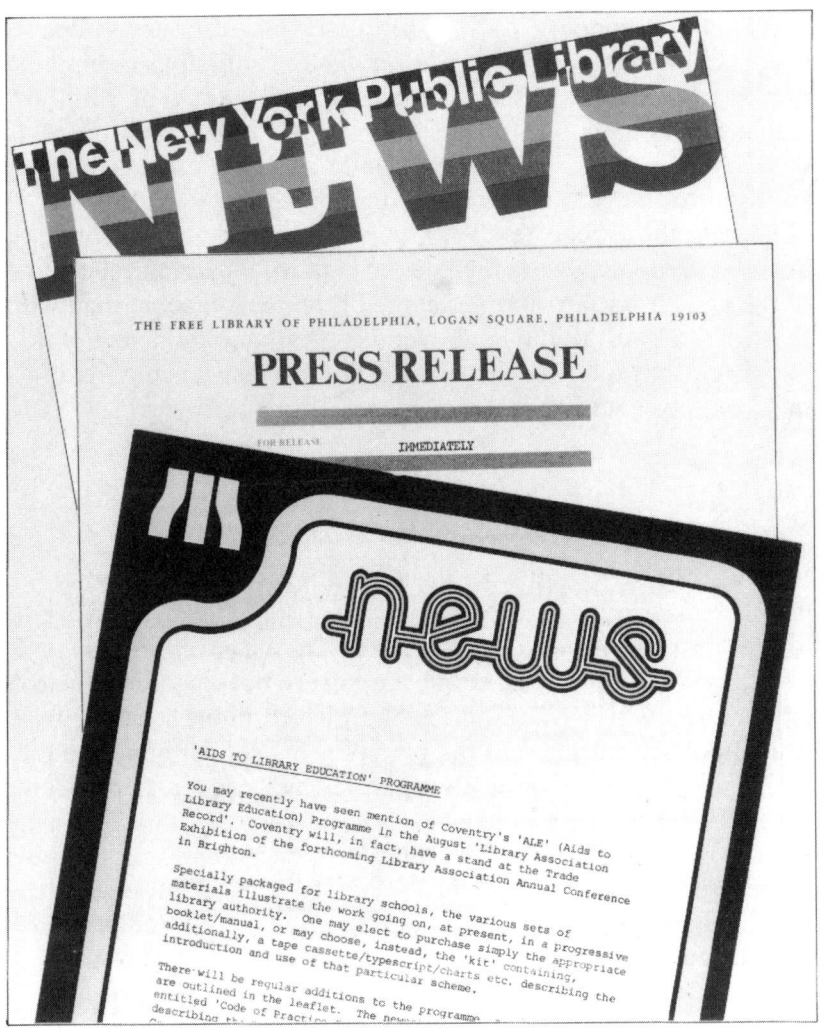

Styles in news release stationery: The New York Public Library, The Free Library of Philadelphia, City of Coventry Libraries.

It is a false economy to use poor-quality paper for news releases because, between leaving the library and eventually reaching the printer, a release will have to take a fair amount of handling. Equally, it is unwise to send carbon copies rather than properly duplicated releases. Carbons look and feel unprofessional and are an insult to the journalists receiving them.

To help those reporters who may require further information, the release should always include the name of the library, the name of the chief librarian, and the name of the person concerned with the story, as well as day and evening telephone numbers. Newspapers do not keep normal office hours so an evening contact number is of some importance.

Photographs

If photographs are sent with a release it is essential to identify the people appearing in them. A simple left-to-right listing is sufficient for this purpose. As with headlines, most newspapers provide their own captions to pictures, so all the library need do is to enclose information which will describe the picture in an accurate way. This should be attached to the picture using rubber gum or adhesive tape so that it can be easily separated by the journalist at a later date. Photographs are expensive to produce and it is uneconomical to send them to all and sundry unless you confidently expect them to be used. It is also wasteful to damage those that are sent by folding them, writing on the back in ballpoint pen and/or by the use of pins and paperclips.

By paying attention to the matters discussed above most librarians should be able to produce a clear, concise communication, which is what a good press release ought to be. Such a communication is much more likely to be used by busy journalists. Thus, the turgid prose of our retirement story can become a crisp and usable release:

NEWS FROM BIBLIOVILLE PUBLIC LIBRARY
Stenton Road, Biblioville, BV2 1AX,
Tel. 1290 (STD Code 0631)

Chief Librarian T Jenner BA MA(Lib) ALA

FOR RELEASE IMMEDIATELY

£50 CHEQUE FOR LIBRARY CARETAKER

Mr. Ted Lister, aged 66, who has worked as a caretaker for the Biblioville library service for 50 years, was today presented with a cheque for £50 in recognition of his service.

At a ceremony attended by library staff, Chief Librarian Thomas Jenner thanked Mr. Lister for his devoted service and said that over the years he must have seen many changes in library buildings.

Mr. Lister is one of the library's oldest caretakers and still remembers one of Biblioville's first librarians Edward Latham. A man who would personally inspect the quality of a caretaker's work.

Ends   1.9.79.

For further information contact:
B.D. Fletcher,
Information Officer,
Biblioville Public Library
Tel. 1290 or 3456 (Evenings)

Distribution

The distribution of press releases needs as much thought as their production. It is essential to maintain an up-to-date mailing and distribution list. It is wasteful to send material to papers or editors that have moved on; it is also bad public relations for it creates an image of the library as an inefficient and out-of-touch organization. The size of this problem was brought home to the writer when, as editor of *The Assistant Librarian,* he regularly received redirected releases from as many as three previous editors. At the same time, it is important to keep up with new publications and to be in touch with developments in local, neighbourhood, and community papers.

If possible, a press release should be sent to a named journalist rather than simply to 'the editor'. For example, if the library produces a booklet on pop music it is sensible to send a copy, together with a news release, to writers who specialize in that particular field. Use should also be made of the large number of hobby and specialist journals whenever a library is promoting an activity or publication related to the interests of their readers.

Timing

The timing of a press release also requires careful consideration. If a release is being sent to a monthly journal, it should be remembered that these often have a long press date. It is unrealistic to send out a release to these papers only a week or so before your event and expect it to be used. The journal will have already been 'put to bed'. If a release is intended for a weekly paper appearing, as most of them do, on Thursday or Friday it is best to send the release to arrive on Monday or Tuesday, giving the editor plenty of time to consider the story. If it arrives at the last moment it will be competing with urgent items of late news.

Even if a librarian follows all the rules indicated above, not every release he or she issues will appear in public print. This should not deter the public-relations-oriented librarian from supplying the press with information, always providing that the subject is worth writing and reading about. It can be helpful to study national and local papers to find out what type of story they favour and to ascertain their editorial likes and dislikes. Above all, it is essential to develop a news sense.

Libraries and librarians can and do provide a wide variety of newsworthy activities. These need not always be major events like the opening of a new building; lesser happenings, such as staff retirements, new equipment and services, visiting dignitaries, exhibitions and events, are all of interest and should receive coverage if presented in the right way. With the right approach, most library authorities should be able to appear in the press at least once a week.

Press contact

The press will sometimes contact a library as the result of a press release. A journalist may telephone for further details or to clear up a point. Ideally, the librarian should be able to give the information at the time, but it may be necessary to check a fact or figure. If you are unable to answer a point of detail immediately, arrange to call back rather than guess — but do keep to a time. Time is especially important for reporters working to an editorial deadline.

At other times, the press may contact a librarian, unprompted by a release. He or she may be asked to comment on some current issue or topic. In such circumstances, it is a fine matter of judgement as to just what to say and this will of course vary with the precise circumstances. Suffice it to say that 'no comment' should only be used as a last report. Faced with an enquiring journalist, the general rule for a librarian is to be calm and factual.

Press conferences

Other aspects of press relations include press conferences, press visits, letters to the editor and feature articles.

For the average public library a press conference is a rare event. A conference might be held in connection with a new building or an important new service. It is most likely that the detailed arrangements for such an event will be made by the local authority's Public Relations Department, but it is helpful if the librarian is at least aware of some of the procedures involved.

Timing a press conference requires careful consideration. In particular, it is important to choose a time and day when, as far as it is possible to judge in advance, the library event will not clash with other similar activities likely to be of interest to the press. For journalists working to a daily deadline, the time of day can be important. Most professional PR people advise holding press conferences between 11 and 12 o'clock in the morning, or between 2 and 3 in the afternoon.

Once the location, date, and time of the conference have been chosen, the invitations can be sent out. Ideally, these should be distributed so as to arrive 10 to 14 days before the event. This gives journalists a chance to reply, thus providing a rough idea of the numbers likely to attend, an important point if catering arrangements are to be made. There will always be interested journalists or organizations unable to attend for one reason or another and these should be sent copies of any material distributed at the conference.

Letters

The 'Letters' section carried by most papers can sometimes provide a librarian with an opportunity to promote the library service. For example, if a reader has written to a paper requesting information on this or that topic, it is a good idea for the library to provide it via the same 'Letters' column. On other occasions, the librarian may feel inclined to respond to criticism of the library's policies or services. In some authorities, when an important policy issue is under discussion, the chairperson of the appropriate committee may wish to sign the letter, but in most cases it will in fact be written by the chief librarian or a senior member of staff.

It is sometimes useful to telephone the editor concerned if a critical letter appears, asking for space to reply. However, do heed the caution about corrections given earlier. Sometimes an editor will send a copy of a critical letter to the library so that the letter and any explanation can appear together. If the criticism is justified (and there will be times when it is) the librarian should apologize and promise to do better in the future. If there is a reasonable explanation, it should be put clearly and succinctly avoiding the use of jargon, as always. Newspapers are at liberty to edit letters in the same way that they edit other material. Often this can improve the final result but on occasions it can make a nonsense of an argument. If you do not want your letter to appear in a truncated version, say so — though this may of course increase the risk of its not appearing at all.

Library features

Very occasionally, a librarian may be asked to supply a feature article for a paper or a journal. For example, a few years ago a London reference librarian was asked to prepare a series on local history to appear in a neighbourhood 'shopping paper'. Normally, though, librarians have to offer their services. Book and record reviews, together with articles on local history, are obvious and suitable outlets for librarians with critical and journalistic skills. The general press need not always be the target for such efforts; a number of librarians writing in a personal capacity have managed to place articles on the literature of a subject in a magazine dealing with one of their pet interests. The special expertise of subject librarians can also be used to effect in a wide range of specialist journals. Full-scale features will, more often than not, be written by reporters whose interest has been aroused by a librarian. The job of the librarian is to sow the seed of that interest. This means developing a continuing and cooperative working relationship with journalists over a period of months rather than days.

By and large, journalists prefer to work with others of the same profession and some of the larger libraries in the United States have press professionals working within their Public Relations Departments. For example, the Free Library of Philadelphia, which has been particularly successful in placing feature articles, has two journalists on its PR staff of eight. There is no doubt that such shared professional experience helps a library in its relations with the press.

It would be unrealistic, at the present time, to expect many British libraries to appoint journalists to PR posts, though some are to be found in local authority Public Relations Departments. However, a librarian can gain the respect and the assistance of the press if he or she takes a little time and trouble to find out about its problems and procedures and then makes sure that the library keep them in mind when organizing press activities.

REFERENCE

1 Black, S *Practical public relations* 3rd ed., Pitman, 1970.

Chapter 7
Radio and Television

Radio and television provide the public librarian with further outlets for public relations material. Indeed, most of the librarians that I interviewed in the United States felt that the broadcasting media were more effective than paper and print in spreading the word for libraries. Local stations are particularly important. Local radio stations are now fairly common in Britain and their number is certain to increase in the next few years. There will then be further opportunities for effective library promotion.

Radio is an especially good medium for reaching the non-user. In its report on services to the disadvantaged, the Department of Education and Science emphasized the potential of radio: '. . . they [library authorities] should be much more prepared to publicize the library in a variety of ways: on local official signboards, through local papers, and *especially local radio*' (my emphasis).[1]

Local radio stations

The local library and the local radio station, especially if it is a BBC station, have much in common. They are both public services dedicated to the communication of information and ideas and concerned with serving the needs of the local community. This common philosophy has led to a great deal of fruitful cooperation between local libraries and local BBC stations. Thus, local libraries have helped stations organize their archives and indeed played a part in the radio stations' own public relations activities. Nottingham public libraries, for example, have housed displays for the local station and sold BBC records through library service points.

Many libraries provide background material for programmes and a number have supplied stations with quiz questions and answers. Both BBC and ILR (Independent Local Radio) stations use library buildings to house satellite studios. As with press relations, it is important for the library to be recognized by the radio station's staff as the place to go for professional help and reliable information.

In all its pre-programme publicity for the 1979 *Roadshow Info* programmes the BBC stressed the role that the public library had to play in the project. More recently, the Corporation asked libraries to act as local back-up agencies in connection with the *Speak for Yourself* Series designed for people whose language and culture was not English. This is a welcome recognition by network broadcasters of the vital role of the public library in the community.

The kind of cooperation mentioned above increases the contact between professional broadcasters and professional librarians. This helps develop a mutual trust and understanding which can only benefit a library service in its attempts to get on the air. It is important to make contact, not just with station managers, but also with individual producers and presenters. In the writer's experience, professional broadcasters have always shown a genuine interest in library activities, often expressing surprise at the range and quality of service offered by the library profession. In most cases, if the library is willing to talk to a local BBC station its personnel are willing to listen.

The commercial ILR stations appear to be less interested although the programme requirements set by the IBA for ILR (and included in the contract particulars for new ILR franchises) state that: 'The authority lays special emphasis on the local nature of the services to be provided, and on their close identity with the areas they serve'.[2] The IBA can also specify a minimum average amount of locally originated programming.

All this may come as a surprise to people who listen to ILR stations (with the exception of the news station, LBC). The present situation may change, however, if the wish of the Annan Committee[3] for local stations operated by non-profit distributing trusts is fulfilled.

Libraries on the air

There are a number of ways in which a library service can be publicized and promoted on the air. Like the press, radio is a news medium and local radio stations should be kept informed of library news. Radio stations should be sent press releases, but a press release written for newspapers may not be suitable for broadcasting purposes. If possible, local radio should be sent special versions of news releases. In the small stations, in particular, an announcer may come to the material 'cold', so it is especially important to avoid complicated sentence structures and tongue-twisting words. One should adopt an informal style appropriate for the medium. It is also useful to give the phonetic spelling of uncommon or difficult names.

Major library news such as the opening of a new central library will nearly always receive coverage, but when sending 'routine' items it is probably best for the library to pick a slow news time, in so far as that can be ascertained. In any case, it is always wise to avoid clashing with other major happenings in the locality.

BBC radio stations are normally willing to publicize library events in 'What's on' and 'Community noticeboard' type programmes. Though the BBC does not guarantee to broadcast the information supplied, many of its local stations issue 'What's on' script forms. These can be completed by local organizations, including libraries, and sent to the station 'at the very latest *two* days before the event'. Guaranteed spots can, of course, be paid for on the commercial ILR stations.

A library authority may be able to place guests on talk shows or on the ubiquitous 'phone-in' programmes. Broadcasters and, one suspects, listeners have mixed feelings about the 'phone-in' format. Some love them, some hate them. On some local stations they appear to form a significant part of the schedules and there is little doubt that a librarian who appears on a good 'phone-in' will receive a public view of the library service. Just how representative that view is, is another matter. Some librarians who have shared a 'phone-in' with other guests have been disappointed not to receive a large number of calls. This does not really matter providing the host has asked enough questions. For, even if the librarian receives few calls, there will still be a large number of people listening to the programme as a whole.

Sound techniques

If you are approached by a radio station to appear on a 'phone-in' or any other kind of show, you should ask the following questions:

>What is the programme?
>How long is the programme?
>For how long do you expect me to speak?
>Is the programme 'live' or recorded?
>What is known about the programme's audience?
>Am I the only guest or will I be part of a panel?
>Who is the interviewer?
>What kind of questions will I be asked?

It is unlikely that you will receive the kind of treatment sometimes reserved for evasive politicians but you do need to be well prepared. The answers you receive to the questions given above should help make your preparation more adequate and relevant. Occasionally, you may be given very little time to prepare for a broadcast, but even if you only have minutes rather than months, consideration of some of the following points will prove useful.

When planning what to say, do remember that broadcasters deal in minutes and seconds. There will not be time for you to explain everything about your library, its history, and services. Even if there was, it is doubtful if the radio audience would take it all in. So, with the background information about the programme in mind plan to communicate the library message so that you make just two or three key points, at the most. Try also to anticipate the 'angle' that will be put on your contribution.

Don't use library jargon; if you do slip into it, explain what you mean in everyday language. It is a sound technique, in more ways than one, to try and paint pictures in the listener's mind. Thus, rather than talking about the 'international availability of books through library interlending services', tell your audience that it is possible for someone using a local library to borrow a book from the Lenin Library in Moscow.

Radio and Television 73

It is often said, and experience tends to support the view, that the first visit to a radio studio is a frightening experience but, for the writer, it was the smallness of local radio studios that was the most surprising feature of his first visit. In any case, it is best to get the feel of a studio before broadcasting. This will enable you to concentrate on what you are going to say and to ignore the activities of the people at work behind the glass panel.

If you are offered the choice, arrange to be interviewed in your own familiar surroundings, at home or in the library office. If you are given this facility, try to make life easier for the broadcaster by not allowing the telephone to ring or children to burst into the room.

If you are recorded, do not expect to hear all your words of wisdom in the subsequent broadcast. However, the young lady from Camden library who had her 20-minute contribution cut to 25 seconds by Capital Radio seems, on the surface, to have been rather badly treated.[4] On the whole, interviewers treat you fairly and do not want to trick you. Certainly, many people think that they obtain fairer treatment at the hands of local broadcasters than from the local press.

A great deal has been written about the techniques to be applied to radio and television interviews and, indeed, there appears to be a minor industry developing in training people to deal with the media. Most of these training courses employ media personalities and are very expensive. One organization, for example, offers a self-study course on 'how to handle a radio interview'. The 'study pack' includes a 28-minute sound cassette, a set of 67 slides, and a checklist for going on radio. With VAT, this course would cost the aspiring broadcaster over £100.

Some local authorities have sent their staff on media training courses, but I doubt if many librarians have had the benefit of such training. I cannot pretend to offer such a course, but the paragraphs above and those which follow do include a few tips on broadcasting which have been given to the writer by media professionals and librarians, both in Britain and America.

Act naturally

Perhaps the key piece of advice is to be natural. Do not, for instance, put on an accent. Its falseness will only be magnified by the microphone. If your preparation leads you to suspect that you will be asked detailed facts and figures, write them down and take them with you to the studio but never simply read a reply to a question, as this will sound stilted and unnatural.

It is vital that you concentrate on your interviewer and listen carefully to her or his questions. When you reply, try to think of yourself as talking to just one or a few people, not to an audience of 70,000 or whatever the local station achieves. Many people facing the microphone for the first time, and indeed many professional broadcasters, find it useful to think of the microphone as the person they are talking to. You must think about what you are actually saying and think 'talk' words. The spoken vocabulary is very different from the written and radio is a medium that uses talk. Many librarians, and perhaps some broadcasters, may be a little surprised at one station manager's advice to 'forget the rules of grammar'.

Even though you cannot be seen by your audience, smile and move your hands and body if that is the way you normally talk. This will help you give a natural and spontaneous performance.

Many novice broadcasters are afraid that they will 'dry up', especially if they are faced with a live interview. It is, however, your interviewer's job to worry about that and a good professional broadcaster will keep things going. All in all, if you know your subject (and you should not be in the studio if you don't!) there is very little in a radio interview to give the competent professional librarian cause for concern.

Library programmes

A few years ago, I wrote that radio station managers 'have yet to be convinced that a library programme as such is good radio.'[5] Although many managers today still favour the magazine programme which simply includes library items, there have been a number of regular library programmes in the UK. Hampshire County Library, for example, acquired a faithful following for its programme on BBC Radio Solent, while Birmingham Public Library's *On the shelf* featured such luminaries as Robert Dougall, Charlton Heston, and David Frost. As previously mentioned, celebrities are always a certain way to attract interest in a library activity. Recently, *On the shelf* became part of a magazine programme. It is now broadcast every fortnight in BBC Radio Birmingham's *Time Off* show.

There is a rather longer tradition of local radio and library programmes in the United States. New York Public Library produces no less than five radio shows. These include a panel programme, *Teenage book talk,* and a chat show hosted by the library's director of public relations. New York Public Library also makes use of celebrities, for example, Eartha Kitt, who hosted a programme about the Schomburg collection of black studies material. Detroit Public Library runs a *Meet the author show* and a number of libraries use the quiz show format.

Apart from regular library programmes, a number of stations have featured library documentaries. On this side of the Atlantic one can cite BBC Radio Nottingham's audio guide to the city's new Central Library and BBC Radio Humberside's *Behind the scenes* look at the county library service. So, some librarians have managed to avoid what broadcasters term the 'turn off factor' and have found a successful formula for a library programme. It is perhaps surprising that local stations have not adapted BBC Radio Four's *Enquire within* for local use, and the writer is still convinced that there is room for a good book preview programme.

Some librarian broadcasters have been schooled in the techniques of microphone writing and presentation, by members of the local station's staff. In a number of cases, if practice has not made perfect it has certainly improved performance. Writing, producing, and performing in a radio programme means working within rigid time constraints. It also means forgetting such things as the library's management hierarchy. In one early English library programme the participants were solemnly introduced by their library title. To do this is a waste of precious time. Listeners are just not interested in the fact that Ms X is the technical services officer at

Little-Chudleigh-in-the-Marsh — even if they know what a technical services officer is. Beware, too, of over-scripting a programme so that the final result is stilted and lacking that vital spark of spontaneity.

Advance publicity

Both the library and the radio station will want an audience for the library programme, so the programme itself should be publicized and promoted. An obvious place to advertise the show is in the library itself. At least, users should be informed that their library is on the air. Birmingham Public Library go one better and actually relay the programme in library service points. That authority also keeps their staff informed about the programme by the production of a newsheet entitled *Over to you* 'News about the BPL radio programme'.

Libraries and librarians can also make guest appearances on other specialist programmes, be they aimed at women, gardeners, anglers, backpackers, or whatever. It is particularly important to appear on programmes intended for ethnic minorities. Most of the BBC stations feature programmes in minority languages and the library service should make efforts to contact the producers concerned. This is made easier, of course, if the library employs a liaison officer for ethnic communities who has command of one or more of the ethnic languages.

Writing in the library press a few years back, one radio station manager wrote: 'we feature book reviews and interviews across a wide range of output. They appear in news programmes, and specialized features, such as those devoted to motoring, sea sports, folk music, etc.'[6] If you find yourself appearing in such a magazine format, do not be surprised if your contribution is interspersed with gramophone records. Librarians can also of course appear in their own right because of a personal interest or achievement. Such publicity is normally useful and it is worthwhile informing stations about staff who have done something of note.

Although most of a public library's broadcast PR will be through local stations, with a degree of creativity it is often possible to gain

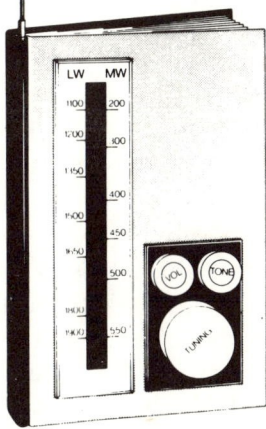

 **BIRMINGHAM PUBLIC LIBRARIES**

BBC RADIO BIRMINGHAM

ON THE SHELF
A PROGRAMME ABOUT BOOKS AND LIBRARIES

Tune in to 206m (1457 kHz) or 95·6 VHF

Sunday 15 January, 4·33pm.
    (repeat Thursday 19 January, 6·30pm.)

Sunday 12 February, 4·33pm.
    (repeat Thursday 16 February, 6·30pm.)

Sunday 12 March, 4·33pm.
    (repeat Thursday 16 March, 6·30pm.)

A leaflet designed to publicize Birmingham Public Library's *On the shelf*. An Urdu language version was also produced to attract listeners from the Indian community.

at least a mention on network programmes, such as *You and yours*, *In touch*, *Moneybox*, and the like. It is worth keeping the producers of these programmes informed about any library activity relevant to the interests of their listeners.

Public service announcements

Library Public Service Announcements (PSAs) are fairly common on radio in the United States. A PSA has been defined as a 'carefully constructed message, usually no more than 60 seconds in length, that succinctly provides the public with information about specific or general materials, services, and programs of your library'.[7] There are many more broadcasting outlets in the United States than in Great Britain and some broadcasters feel that because of the demand for air space, stations in this country would be overwhelmed if they went into the PSA business. However, BBC Radio London has experimented with PSAs, though not as yet on behalf of libraries.

ATV, the Midlands commercial television company, has also run a pilot project. Under its scheme, which has so far been restricted to voluntary organizations, groups ask to be given a week on ATV, in which to tell people about their good works or services. If a group is selected, they go to ATV's studios and videotape a simple message. The company guarantees five showings in the week, although the precise timing is decided by ATV presenters who put the message on the air at suitable moments between programmes, for example when the local company is waiting to rejoin the network.

Public service announcements might be one way for a library to reach the estimated 17 million people[8] who listen to local commercial radio. The PSA is well suited to the pop — news — jingle — weather — pop format of the commercial stations and a number showed interest when the idea was put to them.[9]

Some examples of PSAs are included in this chapter and from these it should be clear that time is a major consideration when producing a PSA for broadcasting. At the most, there will be 60

CITY OF PHILADELPHIA

THE FREE LIBRARY OF PHILADELPHIA
LOGAN SQUARE
PHILADELPHIA, PA. 19103

RADIO/TV SPOT ANNOUNCEMENT

BEGIN: IMMEDIATELY

END: AT WILL

10 SECONDS

    Want to know how to spell a word? Have a problem in punctuation? Need a foreign address? Call General Information at the Free Library of Philadelphia. MU 6-5322.

RADIO/TV SPOT ANNOUNCEMENT

BEGIN: IMMEDIATELY

END: AT WILL

30 SECONDS

    Want to know how to spell a word? Need a quotation from Shakespeare or the address of the firm that manufactured your refrigerator. How about a dictionary definition? Call General Information at the Free Library of Philadelphia. MU 6-5322. Reference librarians are at the phones during library hours to give you information you need for your business, job, school or homemaking. When you need information think General Information. MU 6-5322.

           #   #   #   #

8/11/76

Art Milner
Information Officer
Public Relations Department
MU 6-5425

Examples of spot announcements.

seconds in which to put the library's message across, sometimes only 10. The library will then have to be absolutely clear as to what it wants to say, and there will only be time to make one, perhaps two, very basic points. A 60-second PSA will probably be too long for many stations, so it is wise to give a station a choice by submitting (say) 30 and 60-second versions of a message. The first few words of the PSA should be used to arrest the listener's attention, so do not make your main points then but give the vital information a little later. If possible, give it twice by saying the same thing in different words.

A number of American public librarians have produced rule-of-thumb guides to PSA timing. They do not all agree the precise figures but the translation of words into seconds seems to fall in the following range:

10 secs	20 – 25 words
20 secs	40 – 50 words
30 secs	60 – 75 words
60 secs	125 – 150 words.

Public service announcements to be used on television need to be visually interesting and care should be taken in the preparation of the slide or animation used to complement the verbal message.

A few years ago, the New York Public Library ran a 30-second television PSA entitled *The Magic Card*. This featured a lively animation and the message: 'Your New York Public Library card when stamped ... becomes a magic card. It becomes puppet shows, records, cassettes, ... books ... magic shows ... storytelling hours ... plays ... all yours ... all free. Get a magic card at any branch library. To find out where to get yours, call 790—6161'.

Such was the impact of this PSA that the telephone company complained that their circuits were becoming overloaded. The telephone number was deleted and the spot redistributed to stations. It was then used continuously until it was noted that the expiry date on the 'magic card' was out of date!

New York's experience with the 'magic card' demonstrates the power of television as a communications medium but it also shows the need for a library to be prepared for the size of response that television can produce. In this case it was the telephone company

Radio & Television Spots

Brooklyn Public Library Grand Army Plaza, Brooklyn, N.Y. 11238

Script: Spanish Information Center
Length: 20 sec.
Week of: March 28 - April 3, 1978

Mar. 13, 1978

April 3 is a grand day for all Spanish speaking Brooklynites! It's the gala opening of El Centro, the Spanish language library and information center, located on the lower level of the Williamsburgh Library, Division at Marcy Avenue. There will be films, speakers, stories and a whole lot of fanfare all day long. A Spanish speaking staff is always available. Festivities begin at 1 and all is free.

tel.: 387-6391

¡El 3 de abril será un gran día para la gente de Brooklyn! Se abrirá EL CENTRO HISPANO DE INFORMACION, una biblioteca bilingue donde hay libros para todos los cuales pueden ser prestados. Además ofrece información para continuar la educación y buscar empleo. El Centro está localizado en la biblioteca pública en Williamsburgh, 240 Division Avenue (Marcy y Division). Habrán películas, oradores, cuentos, y mucho más. Los empleados hablan español. Las festividades empiezan a la una de la tarde hasta las ocho, y todo es gratuito. ¡Aprovechese de estos nuevos beneficios!

Example of spot announcement: PSA issued by Brooklyn Public Library reflects the multi-cultural nature of the radio audience.

82   *The Visible Library*

that was overwhelmed, but before any library promotes a service it should make sure it can meet the demand that it hopes to create.

Professional radio and television spots are expensive to produce and library authorities may well think of mounting a broadcasting campaign on a cooperative basis. In the late 1960s Betty Rice, a private library public relations consultant, was involved in the production of a set of radio and television spots for a cooperative of libraries in New York State. Part of this campaign was the library song which was played and sung in their own styles by artists, such as Mitch Miller, Eddy Arnold, and the Tokens. Also included in this project was an entertaining piece by Woody Allen. As we shall see later, The American Library Association also provides television and radio stations with library spot announcements.

Television

In Britain, television is a national and to some extent a regional medium of communication. It is, therefore, difficult for libraries or librarians to obtain much air time. Of course, local libraries supply information to stations, and major library happenings such as a royal visit will almost certainly be covered by the BBC and IBA regional stations. No library in this country has yet followed the example of those in America that are actually producing programmes for television. If the fourth television channel had, as the Annan report[3] advocated, been given to an 'open' broadcasting authority rather than to ITV, local authorities might well have been able to produce programmes for it — but for the moment that is not to be. Cable television may also provide some opportunities in the future, as may some of the ideas advocated by the community communications organization, Com. Com.

Appearing on television

Even though a television appearance is something that may only happen very rarely to the average librarian, a few tips may not come amiss. For those who want more, there are a number of books available and two titles are given at the end of the chapter.[10] First, remember that television is an informal medium and though a total audience may number millions, your communication is by and large going out to one or a few people watching in their own homes. The style adopted should be appropriate for that kind of communication, rather than one that might be used for addressing a multitude.

Some of the basic rules of public communication apply. You should not use jargon and you should pay some attention to your appearance. As a general rule you should wear comfortable clothes, but avoid stripes or checks because they have a strange effect on television cameras. The make-up team will probably make sure that you do not have any stray hair, open flies, smudged mascara, or whatever, but it is best to check in a mirror before facing the camera. Flashy, light-reflecting jewellery can be very distracting to the viewer and should be avoided.

It is quite permissible to take notes into a studio, though of course you should not read from them. However, it is far better to refer to notes to clarify a fact or figure rather than to make it up. Finally, do not pay attention to the camera; even professional broadcasters sometimes have difficulty in ascertaining which camera is 'on' at any particular time. Anyone who is not used to a television studio is best advised to look at the interviewer and let the director worry about the shots. Talking of which, do not be too embarrassed to ask the director to concentrate on your best side in terms of profile. Like it or not, television is partly about creating impressions, and if you feel one side of your face is going to create a better impression than the other, use it — though within limits.

Evaluating the results

Librarians should examine their broadcasting activities as carefully and as critically as they would look at other aspects of their library service and organization. It is still rather too easy to become carried away with the glamour of broadcasting, but it is not enough simply to appear on radio or television, or even to produce a programme. Librarians should watch and listen to recordings of their broadcasts and attempt to evaluate their impact by answering the following questions honestly:

Was the style and approach appropriate for the programme's audience?
Was it clear who/what the programme was for?
How successful was the programme in achieving its aims?
If the programme failed, why?

A programme intended to inform an audience can, for example, fail because too much information is packed into too short a period of time.

When asking these questions, you should also seriously consider if the objectives of the programme could have been better achieved via another medium. Last, but by no means least, honestly consider whether or not the programme seemed professional. This means comparing the library's efforts with other productions available to the listener or viewer.

If members of a library service can give a positive response to most of the questions asked above, then their library service is well on the way to making effective use of two of the most powerful methods of communication available — radio and television.

NOTES AND REFERENCES

1. Department of Education and Science. *The libraries' choice: report of the working party on library service to the disadvantaged,* HMSO, 1978.
2. *Particulars of Independent Local Radio contract. Coventry,* IBA, 1978.
3. *Report of the Committee on the Future of Broadcasting* (The Annan Report), *HMSO,* 1977.
4. Hedges, C 'On being interviewed for Capital or I could be another Angela Rippon if I didn't keep falling off the radio', *Newsletter No. 80 for Camden Libraries and Arts Staff,* June 1979.
5. Usherwood, R C 'Library public relations: an introduction' in Holroyd, G (ed.) *Studies in library management* 2 Bingley, 1974.
6. Gunnell, R 'Radio Brighton and Hove' letter, *Assistant Librarian* 64 (8), August 1971.
7. Kohn R 'PSA writing' in Moran, I (*comp.*) *The library public relations recipe book,* Public Relations Section, Library Administration Division, American Library Association, 1978.
8. *Television and radio 1979; guide to independent television and independent local radio,* IBA, 1978.

9 See: Kendall, M 'Public libraries and local radio stations in Britain'. A study submitted in partial fulfilment of the requirements for the degree of Master of Arts in Librarianship at the University of Sheffield, 1979, (unpublished).
10 See, for example:
Bland, M *You're on next! How to survive on television and radio,* Kogan Page, 1979.
Brand, J *Hello, good evening and welcome: a guide to being interviewed on television and radio,* Shaw & Sons, 1977.

Chapter 8
Public Speaking

Most public librarians, at some time in their career, will be asked to speak in public. The invitation may come from the local church group asking the librarian to talk to an afternoon meeting, or from a professional association seeking a speaker for a national conference. The good public speaker should be equally at home talking to a dozen or so people in a draughty village hall or addressing an audience of several hundreds in a large conference auditorium. In both cases, and in all conditions in between, it is essential for the librarian speaker to prepare for the event.

Preparation

There are a number of things that every speaker should check before he or she starts the actual job of writing a talk or paper. Some of these should have been covered in the letter of invitation but this will not always be the case.

What then should you do after receiving an invitation to speak? First and foremost you should check when and where you are expected to perform, and for how long you are expected to be on your feet. You should also find out if you will be expected to answer questions. It is also useful to know where you are appearing in a programme of events. If it is a programme involving more than one person, you should ascertain who the other contributors are going to be and who will act as the chairperson for your session.

There are some very practical matters that should be on every speaker's checklist. You should find out well in advance how to reach the venue and if you are going to be met at the station or airport. If travelling by car, be sure to obtain a map and details of one-way systems and parking facilities. Practical questions regarding the hall or auditorium also need to be asked. You must check if the organization can provide the equipment you might require for your presentation. Will there be a lectern, overhead projector, and/or the right kind of slide projector?

Identify your audience

Also, if appropriate, ask the organizers to send you a copy of their annual report and/or calendar of events. This can help you obtain a 'feel' of an organization and its interests. A reference in your talk to an earlier happening or to one of their interests indicates to an audience that you are interested in their activities. Politicians are very adept at using this technique. Witness how President Carter won over an audience in north-east England by using the phrase 'hawa the lads' — the rallying cry for the local football team. Always find out about the audience you will be talking to. You will need to know its likely size and its composition in terms of age, sex, race and religion. If it is an audience of fellow professionals you will need to be aware of their level of experience.

The same talk presented in the same way to different audiences will not do. Even if you are giving a general talk about the library and its services you should make it relate to the audience in front of you. With an audience of elderly residents local studies material is often of particular interest, while the local Chamber of Trade will probably be interested to learn about your services to industry and commerce. If you are talking to library school students, try to relate your remarks to the programme of studies that they are following.

It is also important to find out if the press will be present. If so, and the occasion is important enough, reporters may require preprints of your paper. Also, with the press present you may feel less free to make off-the-cuff comments.

Expenses

Finally, there is the delicate question of expenses. Sometimes these may be legitimately met from your library's own funds but at other times you may feel that the local authority should not pay. I once spoke following the Annual General Meeting of an organization and it was not until I heard the Hon. Treasurer's report that I realized that my out-of-pocket expenses (not unduly high) would put the organization in the red. Discretion being the better part of valour, I never put in a claim, but since that date I have always attempted to have the matter clarified before the event.

Of course, speakers should not be put in such an embarrassing position, and it is to be hoped that librarians who organize events will, when writing to possible participants, make the position regarding expenses and other matters mentioned above quite clear in their letters of invitation. That, too, is good public relations.

Content

Having assured yourself on such practical matters you can begin to think about writing your presentation. Even if you are one of those gifted people who can talk without notes, some form of written preparation provides the discipline necessary for a well-structured talk. If nothing else, it can reveal the logical development, or otherwise, of your speech. Also, the act of writing is in itself a valuable form of mental preparation. Before writing, you should be clear as to what you hope to achieve by speaking to the particular audience concerned. That is to say that it is just as necessary to define the objective of public speaking as it is for any other form of public relations activity.

As indicated above, the content of a talk should take account of the interests, hopes, and aspirations of the audience, the detail will of course depend on the nature of the topic. In arranging a talk, the advice given to university teachers to — 'tell them what you are going to say — tell them — and then tell them what you have said', is worth considering.

The introduction to a talk is crucial for it forms your initial verbal contact with the audience. Your main argument should then be developed in a logical sequence, and it is important to finish on a strong note. These points are discussed in more detail a little later.

Presentation

The success of a talk or lecture can depend almost as much on its presentation as its content. Many speakers find it useful to rehearse their public speeches. The traditional aids of a mirror and a watch are all that are essential for this, but with the general availability of tape-recorders many now use these as well. Certainly, a tape-recorder can help you ascertain if you suffer from 'the mumbles' or a similar affliction.

With regard to timing you should, within reason, aim to keep within the time allotted to you. Anyone who has been on the receiving end of speeches that have gone on too long knows that they do not encourage one to be favourably disposed towards a speaker or the message contained in his or her speech. Also, as a speaker, it can be very uncomfortable to find yourself talking against the clock. Although rehearsals are valuable, beware of over rehearsing. This can result in a lack of spontaneity in your final and most important performance.

Notes

For many people, notes are the most essential aid for a presentation. The preparation of notes is a very individual activity and the only general rule applicable is to find, and continue to use, a form that is comfortable for you. You should make sure that this format is not too easily disarranged if disaster befalls, and you drop your papers. Many speakers make notes on numbered 5 x 3 inch cards and hold them in the palm of their hand. This seems to work perfectly well. Personally, I use A4 paper fixed in a ring binder. This is not a method I have seen recommended elsewhere but it is one with which I feel comfortable.

Some people make lengthy notes, others just headings. Again, there is no prescribed method. It is, however, not advisable to make notes, lengthy or otherwise, in pencil as they could be difficult to read, especially in artificial light. The main consideration is how you use your notes. It is essential that they do not come between you and your audience.

Even when, no — especially when, a script has been fully prepared for future publication, it is wrong to read from it. The language and construction suitable for publication are not the same as that suitable for speaking. Adjust your language before speaking and never use, unless speaking to fellow-professionals, library jargon, uncommon acronyms or abbreviations, or for that matter abbreviations with more than one meaning. The use of BL (for British Library) may well mystify and confuse a public used to seeing BL in headlines reporting the problems of the British motor industry.

Beginning the talk

When making your presentation, the crucial thing to remember is that for the period of your talk you will be the centre of attention. For the audience you are the personification of the library service. It is a unique opportunity to put the library's message across — make the most of it.

Before any more is said about how to use that opportunity, just a word about dress. I know of one speaker who has a different set of clothes for different types of audience. He has three categories: 'respectable', 'respectable yet arty', and 'arty and dirty'. Generally one should avoid extremes and be neither too showy nor too untidy. Dress can affect the attitude of an audience and it is not productive to alienate them unnecessarily. As a speaker, your job is to please and stimulate them.

Nerves play a part in any speaker's life. Indeed, one can go so far as to suggest that unless a speaker feels a degree of nervous tension before a performance, he or she is not likely to give a very good talk. The challenge is to keep nerves under control, not to let them show, and to use them constructively. The good public speaker uses nervous tension in the same way as an actor or athlete, to give an edge to a performance.

At the start of a speech, in particular, it is important not to let nerves lead you into the trap of talking too fast. Relax for a short while before you perform. Do not start your talk immediately you have been introduced but look at the audience. Make contact. Allow three or four seconds to elapse. This will give you, quite literally, breathing space. It will also allow the audience to cough, adjust and shift their position. Start slowly and clearly.

It is not necessary, as is sometimes thought, to start with a joke. Generally, such devices are best left to experienced public speakers. A joke that falls flat can badly shake the confidence of someone new to the game. However new or inexperienced you are, never apologise for making a speech. You have been invited to talk, so be positive. A speaker who starts with, 'I am not sure quite why I was invited to speak . . .' is likely to provoke a fairly obvious response from an audience. At the very least it will identify the speaker as less than an expert.

Delivery

Once the talk has begun, the speaker's job is to interest the audience and to hold their attention. This can be achieved in a number of ways. The subject itself has, of course, to be relevant and interesting, but even when this is the case people have fairly short spans of attention. A number will start to drift away after about twenty minutes. You must make a conscious effort to speak clearly, to pause where necessary to enable the audience to take in information, to vary the tone of voice, and not to mumble. You should also make an effort to regain the audience's attention throughout your talk. This can be accomplished by a change of pace, a change of subject, or the occasional digression. In addition, the use of an appropriate visual or audio aid at a suitable point can revitalize an audience's interest.

Gestures

A speaker does not convey his or her message by words alone. We know from everyday encounters how gestures can reinforce a message. The good public speaker uses gesture but uses it in moderation. There is only one Magnus Pyke, and one suspects that he is more often remembered, not for what he says, but for the physical gyrations that accompany what he says.

It is best, when talking in public, to behave naturally. If you normally use your hands when speaking, do so on the platform. In any case, be careful not to get your hands, and subsequently your body, in a fixed position by gripping the end of the table or lectern. Not only does this look unattractive but it tends to make you talk down into your notes, resulting in a loss of voice projection and less eye contact with members of the audience.

There is nothing wrong with pointing fingers or even fist-thumping in moderation, provided that such movements are synchronized with the tone of the subject and the modulation of the voice. Other non-verbal signals, such as smiling, can help put your message across. Also, use your eyes and, if the physical conditions allow, look at the eyes of your audience, rather than at the ceiling or out of a window. Eyes, as we all know, communicate a range of feelings, messages, and emotions. When speaking, make sure yours express sincerity, friendship, and authority.

Those of us who have ever sat in an audience may have been annoyed or, even worse, distracted by the mannerisms of a speaker. Know your own mannerisms, be they jingling coins, playing with rings, or nose wiping, and seek to eliminate them from your public performances, likewise verbal mannerisms of the 'er' and 'um' variety.

Audience feedback

The experienced public speaker will also take account of non-verbal signals given by an audience. Posture is one way in which people convey interpersonal attitudes. There is reported to be a picture somewhere of Dr Spock (during his liberal period) addressing an audience of New York policemen. The entire audience, it is said, have their arms folded demonstrating their psychological withdrawal from, and rejection of, the doctor's ideas. Such simple analysis is rarely possible but a good speaker will watch an audience so as to 'read' its attentiveness, attitudes, and emotions.

Ending the talk

Having taken heed of some of these techniques while making your speech it would be a pity to spoil a good performance with a poor ending. A good conclusion is as important as a good beginning. The end of your talk should be carefully planned and constructed and it should come as a natural conclusion to what has gone before. The audience should be aware from your manner and tone of voice that you are 'building' up to a conclusion. Your aim should be to finish smoothly and with authority. I once saw a very distinguished librarian 'conclude' a speech by looking at his watch and saying: 'my time is up so I will finish there'. This he did, leaving his audience in a dissatisfied and uneasy limbo.

Question time

At the end of a talk you will more likely than not be faced with 'question time'. The danger here is that, having finished the formal speech, the speaker relaxes and forgets some of the basic rules of talking to an audience. The impression created by a good speech can sometimes be ruined by a poor performance during the question-and-answer period. A special problem facing public librarians, and other public servants, is that they are often taken to task for the shortcomings of the local authority as a whole. A good chairperson will handle this situation but speakers are not always blessed with good chairpersons. You should avoid being drawn into arguments about the frequency of refuse collection or whatever, and simply refer the questioner to the appropriate office or department.

When dealing with questions that you can answer, always give yourself time to think. Never rush into a reply. Generally, it is advisable to keep answers short and to the point. If a question is a difficult one, it is possible to obtain extra thinking time by asking the questioner to repeat what he or she has said.

If you cannot answer a question never make up an answer or try to bluff your way out of the situation. If it is simply a case of not having facts to hand, arrange to have the necessary information sent to the person concerned. When people make suggestions about the library service, always respond in a positive way. Be firm but fair in rejecting unworkable suggestions, explaining why in plain language. Where a suggestion has potential value, say so. Thank the person making it and promise to take it back for consideration. In fact, do more than promise — do it. The users' or non-users' outlook is often very revealing and public speaking engagements provide an opportunity to listen to, as well as to talk to, a section of the community.

During question time you should attempt to become part of the audience. This allows for a more fruitful exchange of opinions. Such closeness can be achieved by physical means, for example by taking questions sitting down. You should also, if possible, involve the audience in the session. This can be achieved by turning a question back on an audience by saying something like, 'I should like to learn what other people think about this'. Sometimes the question period will suffer from a lack of questions. You can do something to insure against this happening by leaving an obvious gap in your exposition, or by mentioning an idea or topic and saying very little else about it.

Vote of thanks

At the end of the event there will probably be a vote of thanks, or some less formal kind of 'thank you'. Very often the person performing this duty is nervous and this can lead to the lengthy, the boring, and sometimes the hilarious. One gentleman speaker known to the writer received the following accolade from an elderly lady chairperson: 'I must say that every point on which Mr ... has put his finger has given me immense pleasure'. Good public speakers will take such pleasures in their stride and reply with a simple and sincere 'thank you'.

Facing a microphone

In larger halls and conference centres you may be faced with a microphone. Contrary to conservative conventional wisdom, the microphone is not an instrument of the devil but a useful aid to public speaking. One sometimes feels that some speakers think it reflects on their virility to use a microphone. How many of us have attended meetings where a speaker declines to use the microphone and then proceeds to talk, inaudibly to part of the audience? This is not only arrogant and foolish, it is discourteous to people who, at the very least, have invested their time in order to be present.

It is true that the use of a microphone requires a little practice but the techniques required should not be beyond the average intelligent adult. First and foremost, the microphone, like other aids, should not be allowed to come between speaker and audience. Never look at a microphone, always look at the audience. There are two other considerations regarding use of microphones: distance and tone of voice.

As far as the voice is concerned, you should speak as you would if you wanted your voice to carry across a large living-room — that is, to carry about 30 ft. The best distance to stand from a microphone depends very much on the model used. Most people recommend a distance of between 18 and 36 inches but it is always best, if possible, to take the advice of those who know the equipment. As a final test, watch your audience, especially those at the back. If their faces and posture indicate that they have difficulty in hearing you or, alternatively, that their eardrums will be shattered, adjust your distance and power accordingly.

Although it is perhaps more fitting for the question period, an intimate conversational tone can be achieved, even with quite a large audience, by having the microphone moved in close, say to a distance of 9 to 12 inches. Microphones are far less directional than they used to be and it should be possible to traverse about 45 degrees on either side without your message losing its aural clarity.

Publicity handouts

A public meeting often provides a librarian with a useful opportunity to disseminate printed messages as well as aural ones, but you should never distribute your wares until after you have spoken. If people receive handouts, brochures, or other publicity material before you talk to them, there is a danger that they will read them while you are speaking!

A valuable asset

The skill of public speaking is a real public relations asset for any librarian. Public speaking engagements enable the public librarian to make contact with important community organizations. They provide, often quite literally, a platform from which the library message can be promulgated.

Techniques, such as those outlined above, should be included in staff training programmes. Members of staff with a particular talent for public speaking should be encouraged to use it, and all members of staff should at least be made aware of the importance of quality in their public utterances. As we show later, effective speaking is also of value in other situations, such as staff or committee meetings. Speech is in fact a public relations medium which is available to every public library service. Library managers should make the most of it.

Chapter 9
Miscellaneous Methods

This chapter provides a potpourri of public relations methods and techniques. Inclusion does not necessarily imply recommendation. However, in most cases I feel that the ideas are at least worth a try. How such methods are adopted for local use depends on local circumstances and the creativity of the library staff concerned. What follows is not intended to be a complete listing: other ideas are to be found in the rest of the book, but many more exist in the minds of creative-thinking librarians. I should like to hear of any used in your library, successful or otherwise. Now to some methods which I have observed on my actual and vicarious travels.

Bus trips

Perhaps motivated by the fuel crisis, a number of library authorities in the United States have organized bus trips to theatres, museums, or simply to shops. This type of library service has proved to be particularly popular with older library members. In Britain, one or two libraries arrange coach tours to places of local historical interest as an extension of their local studies services.

Some libraries in the USA actually run their own bus services to take people to use libraries. Timetables are published in advance and there are regular pick-up and set-down points. These experiments have only proved partially successful and they probably reflect a lack of adequate public transportation.

Buttons

Buttons and badges have become a popular way of promulgating a message as they are relatively cheap, the metal type costing about £40 for a thousand. Even cheaper is the self-adhesive paper variety, available at around £5 to £6 for the first thousand. Exact prices vary according to size and thickness and whether or not you supply your own artwork. You may well find a supplier in your own area but, failing that, a number of firms can be found advertising in *Exchange & Mart*. Incidentally, the pages of this British institution also include advertisements from organizations specializing in the production of T-shirts, pens, and other promotional products.

Button slogans should be chosen to suit your particular community and/or need. Examples seen by the writer include:

> *I'm a Sutton Library Lover*
> *I got it at the Library*
> *I'm a Public Libraries Research Groupie*
> *Mad about Lad* (That is the Library Administration Division of The American Library Association)
> *I'm a Library Fiend* (complete with graphic fiend)
> *Tie One on for the Library!*

As an alternative to a button, or in addition to it, your library's message can also be inscribed on balloons or car stickers.

Carrier bags

A very practical PR idea, plastic carrier bags not only take the library's message out into the community, but also protect library materials such as books or records. They are not too costly to produce at about £33 plus VAT for 1,000. This cost can be offset by making a small charge for the bag, or by selling advertising space on its side. An eye-catching design and slogan can also be added to good effect. Nassau Library System, for instance, uses the clever catch line: GET CARRIED AWAY — USE YOUR LIBRARY.

One large English firm making carrier bags of all kinds include

A puff for the library! Balloons are a cheap and popular promotional aid. Note too how, in this example from the West Virginia Library Commission, use has been made of the *Star Wars* theme: 'May the force be with you'. (*Photo: Author*)

in their range a number of standard library carriers on to which they can print the name of a particular library authority.

Competitions

Competitions generate interest in a library service and also involve its community. They can also be used to provide further ideas for promotional material. Nottingham Public Library, for example, has produced a poster and a carrier bag based on a design submitted for a 'Design a poster to advertise your library competition'. An even more challenging design competition was run by Kanawha Public Library in the United States. They asked children to 'color the new bookmobile'.

Competitions have for some time been a popular activity in children's libraries. Personally, I have some doubt as to the value of many of these. Too many seem to favour the 'bright' child or the 'good reader'. Reading races, book ladders, and the like may well be counter-productive in that they can frighten away those children who find reading difficult. If you run competitions make sure that they are designed to attract the widest possible range of talent and skills.

Carrier bag based on design for a competition to 'Design a poster' by Nottingham Public Library. (*Photo: Author*)

Computers

Public relations, like other areas of library management, can make use of the computer. Coventry Public Library, for example, has used a computer as part of a campaign to persuade new residents to join the library. The authority's Rent and Rates file was searched to obtain details of people who had recently changed their address and newcomers were sent a package of promotional material.

Public libraries have yet to explore the promotional possibilities of the new information technology. The Videotex systems, for instance, could be utilized by library authorities, individually or cooperatively, to publicize and demonstrate their services. Commercial concerns are already using Prestel in this way.

In addition, the computer can, of course, help with the difficult task of evaluating public relations activities (see Chapter 14), by providing a means of dealing with the complicated calculations required to assess the effectiveness of different approaches to publicity and promotion.

Cooperative PR

British libraries lead the world in terms of library cooperation. However, there have been relatively few attempts at cooperative library public relations. Yet there are a number of advantages to be obtained from cooperative effort, not the least of these being lower cost. The economies to be gained from such things as bulk printing are obvious, and it is surprising that (say) the libraries of London have not worked together to produce posters or banners for display throughout the GLC area. Such publications could be displayed on public transport, stations, or other sites. It would be simple enough to design a poster to incorporate overprinting, where it was felt necessary to identify individual library authorities. Cooperative funding also makes the production and broadcasting of radio and television spots an economic possibility. At the time of going to press it is reported that the Association of London Chief Librarians, together with London Weekend Television, are planning a 15 or 30 second film to be shown as part of the station's community programming.

In 1979, the Sheffield Libraries Coordinating Committee organized a seven-week course on public relations and promotion. This was a real cooperative effort involving the Polytechnic Library, the

Sheffield Public Library, the University Library, and the Postgraduate School of Librarianship and Information Science. The same organisation also mounted a highly successful multi-media exhibit at the 1980 ASLIB/IIS/LA Joint Conference.

Cooperation need not, indeed should not, be restricted to the library profession as such. There is much to be gained from cooperation with other parts of the communications world, such as publishers, booksellers, and broadcasters. The Free Library of Philadelphia has for several years been a major participant in an annual PR event known as Super Sunday. Described as 'a party for the people of Philadelphia', Super Sunday is the result of cooperation between the library, the Academy of Natural Sciences, the Franklin Institute, and a number of other cultural institutions that inhabit the city's Benjamin Franklin Parkway. The occasion has attracted up to half a million people. During the 1974 event the library itself had 35,000 visitors and registered around 1,200 new clients.

There is room for such cooperative efforts in Britain. Apart from the economies of scale to be obtained from such an operation, the very act of cooperation can help a library establish and develop links with important organizations in its community. That in itself is productive public relations.

Correspondence

Letters provide a link between a librarian and members of her or his community. When writing to people, try to avoid an official or formal style. Make contact with your correspondents by giving them a name: 'Dear Mr, Mrs, Ms, or Miss Somebody' is better than 'Dear Sir', or 'Dear Madam'. Of course, librarians are busy people and it is possible for them to waste time searching for the perfect word at the expense of their other work. The best advice on this conflict is to be found in the often quoted words of Sir Ernest Gowers: 'There is a happy mean between being content with the first thing that comes into your head and the craving for perfection that makes a Flaubert spend hours or even days on getting a single sentence to his satisfaction. The article you are paid to produce need not be polished but it must be workmanlike'.[1]

In common with other large organizations, the Directorate of Amenity Services at Lambeth circulates copies of letters sent out from the Directorate. This is not only a useful way of keeping up with colleagues' activities but can also provide a useful check on correspondence style. Look through your library's correspondence from time to time and have a quiet word with those members of staff still replying to 'yours of the 5th inst.'.

Direct mail

Direct mail has been defined as: 'A method of sending unsolicited advertising or promotional material through the post to customers or potential customers at specific named addresses'.[2] As a promotional method, direct mail has the advantage of being a selective and individual way of reaching a user or potential user. It is also a method that is comparatively easy to evaluate. The audience is defined, so cost effectiveness can be measured in terms of direct response.

Through the direct mail technique, a leaflet or booklist produced by a library can be directed to a specific audience. The British Direct Mail Advertising Association will supply, for a charge, lists of people and organizations with specific interests or characteristics. A number of libraries in the United States are using direct mail to disseminate material to specific target audiences, such as senior citizens or mothers-to-be.

The British Post Office maintains on the basis of its research that people enjoy receiving promotional messages through their letter-box, provided that such messages are intelligently tailored for them. Certainly, it is important to monitor the quality of the material distributed in this way. Equally, it is essential to use up-to-date mailing lists.

The Post Office offers rebates on an increasing scale for bulk postings. These could be of use to larger authorities or to authorities combining in a cooperative PR effort. Librarians seeking a blue-print for a library direct mail campaign could do worse than to refer to Blaise Cronin's[3] report of a recent experiment in

Brent, although its conclusions may in fact discourage them from undertaking such activities.

Free samples

During the 1972 National Book Week, the *Serendipity* paperback book containing '20 extracts to wet (sic) your appetite'[4] for books was distributed with some success. It would be quite possible for public library authorities to cooperate to produce another sample collection. This would also of course involve cooperation with the publishing industry. A free sample of this kind might be most effectively distributed in those areas identified as containing a high proportion of people not using library services. The collection would need to be carefully selected, keeping the target group in mind.

Livery

You should use your library transport to take your library's visual identity into the community. Drivers on the highways of West Virginia travelling behind library vehicles are invited to 'BARK IF YOU LIKE LIBRARIES' and told 'ITS ALRIGHT TO SHOUT ABOUT THE LIBRARY'. In addition, the Library Commission's book-mobiles are known as 'THE FLYING BOOK EXPRESS' and 'THE GREAT ORANGE READING MACHINE'.

Even if you prefer the more conventional slogan of 'BOOKS AND INFORMATION', there is no reason why it should not be carried on your library's transport. The transport itself should have distinctive and identifiable colours. Librarians working in authorities striving to develop a corporate identity may well have to go along with the livery designed for the council as a whole. If you can choose your own colour, make sure that it cannot be confused with that used by any other service. One County Library has a fleet of brightly coloured mobile libraries. The only problem is that their colour is very similar to that used by the Post Office and, hence, the library service is often mistaken for a team of telephone engineers!

Transport of Delight.

(*Photo: West Virginia Library Commission*)

West Virginia 'bookmobiles' take the library's message to the freeways. Note the book burst symbol on 'The Great Orange Reading Machine'. (*Photo: Author*)

Memorials

There are echoes of Evelyn Waugh in this fund-raising activity from West Virginia. Part of the text inside the brochure shown below reads: 'Through your library. . . . the gift of knowledge is an eternal way to honour the memory of a departed friend or loved one. . . . Monetary donations of all amounts can be made to your local library to eternalize the memory of a loved one. . . . A gift to the library is an eternal memorial shared by all in the community'.

A piece of PR which not only demonstrates the different funding situation in Britain and America, but also a different way of death.

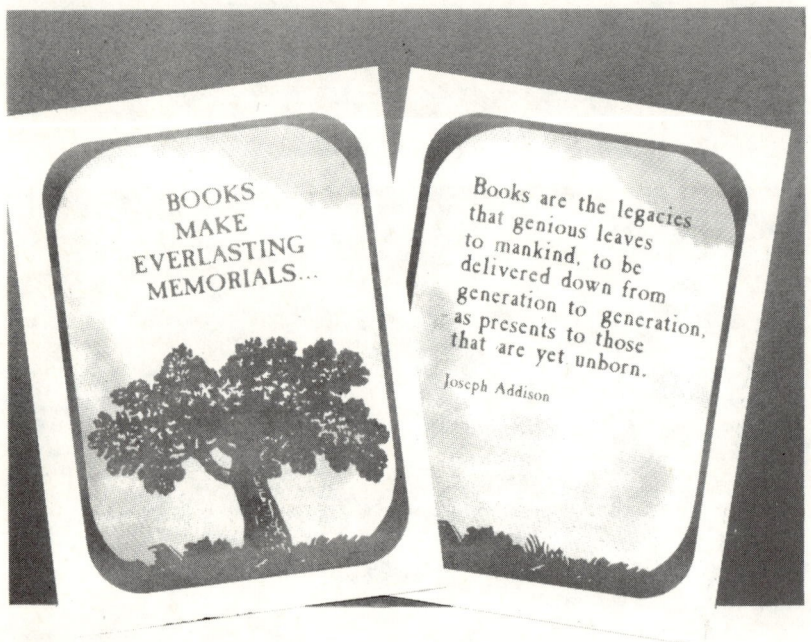

Stock arrangement

Classification schemes can be confusing for library users. A number of libraries are experimenting with arranging stock by alternative means. Bookshop classification or broad topic headings such as 'The home' or 'Transport' have been developed to make library use easier for those who visit a library without a specific title in mind. In some cases, fiction and non-fiction have been grouped together.

At the time of writing, Manchester Public Libraries and East Sussex County Library are known to be experimenting in this way. East Sussex have produced some notes on their scheme. They describe it as 'a new beginning' and say that they hope 'the revised arrangement will be better for those who use libraries at present and that it will encourage others who find the old system too mystifying to make use of their local library'.[5]

Older readers will recall A W McClellan's concept of the reader-centred library providing 'service in depth'. The essential feature of such a library is 'an arrangement allowing a natural and unimpeded movement of the reader from the conditions appropriate to the "diversionary" interests through to those most appropriate to the more "purposive" and thus the more intensely specific'.[6]

Telephone listing

You can help your clients and potential clients contact you by having the library clearly listed in telephone directories. It is well worth paying the small extra charge for multiple listing and entries in the appropriate Yellow Pages. Not everybody wanting to call a library will know the name of the local authority responsible for the service, so just one entry under the local authority is not enough.

Telephone numbers should always be published in full in library publications and correspondence. You should show your STD code as part of the number. The whole of the UK is now on the STD network but you should also include the name of your exchange for the benefit of international callers. Your library number should appear as follows: Sheffield 123456 (STD code 0742).

Tours

Most public libraries of any size receive visits from library schools and other professional groups. However, a large public library should be of interest to more than just professional audiences. A

108   *The Visible Library*

library's programme of guided tours can usefully be expanded to include visits by the general public, local organizations, and other interested parties. The great national libraries do of course provide this kind of facility but it is comparatively rare for public libraries to promote tours for the public at large.

A notable exception to this general rule is the Manchester Public Library which employs a tour organizer to promote, plan, and coordinate visits by professional groups and members of the public. The tour organizer has a public relations background and the tours are widely advertised through schools, galleries, and local organizations. The simple but very creditable objective of the Manchester tour programme is to educate people as to what is available. By all accounts, it has proved to be a successful and rewarding activity for staff and public alike.

During my visit to the United States I joined a public tour of the New York Public Library. Such tours are organized by volunteers from 'The Friends' group. Our guide certainly knew about the library, its services, its history, and finances. Organized very much with the tourist in mind, the cumulative effect of these tours over the years must be a vast reserve of goodwill towards the New York Public Library at local, national, and international levels.

Successful tours do not just happen; they require careful thought and precise planning. Different types of party need different types of tour. A tour organized for the local Chamber of Commerce would not be suitable for a Women's Institute and vice versa. In addition to the type of people involved, you also need to know the number expected on any particular visit. Once the number and composition of a party is known, this information can be communicated to the tour guides.

Whether tour guides are members of the professional staff or volunteers, it is essential that they are fully informed about the library, its history, and activities. Staff or volunteers should not be put in the position of guiding groups without some form of training. One still hears horrendous stories of new members of staff being thrown in at the deep end. It does not help the library's image if guides get lost!

It is crucial to remember that visitors will take in more than simply the information provided about the library and its services.

A publicity leaflet advertising tours of Manchester's Central Library.

They will remember the quality of the organization, the warmth or otherwise of their welcome, and the attitudes of the staff who took them round. If possible, groups should be welcomed by a senior member of staff. It would be unrealistic to expect a busy chief librarian to receive each and every party, but an effort should be made to give visitors a glimpse of top management.

As a matter of practical organization, arrangements should be made for parties to leave their coats, and some 'sitting' time should be included at the beginning, middle, and end of a long tour. If it is possible within the budget, simple refreshments are always welcomed by visitors. Always keep to any prearranged timetable: people on the tour may have other commitments after the visit and it will be spoilt for them if they are worried about being late. In fact, it is a good idea to outline the timetable at the start. The end of the tour is the right time to give visitors the publicity pack mentioned in Chapter 3.

NOTES AND REFERENCES

1 Gowers, E *Complete plain words* 2nd rev. ed., Sir B Fraser, HMSO, 1973.
2 This is the definition adopted by the British Market Research Bureau and used by them in their 1971 study of direct mail.
3 Cronin, B *Direct mail advertising and public library use* (BLR & D Report no 5539), The British Library, 1980.
4 *Serendipity,* The National Book League, 1972.
5 'A New Beginning'. Some notes on the new arrangement at Hangleton Library. Available from Carolyn Jacobs, Hangleton Library, West Way, Hangleton, East Sussex.
6 McClellan, A W *The reader, the library and the book,* Bingley, 1973.

Part Three The Community

> *'It is astonishing how many friends ... there are when such a movement as this is set going, and the voluntary help of all these should be at once enlisted.'*
>
> *Thomas Greenwood* Free Public Libraries, 1887

Chapter 10
Dealing with People

It should never be forgotten that it is people who make up the public in public relations. This chapter is about relationships with people — the internal relationships between management and library employees and the external relationships between librarians and their clients. As we examine these sets of relationships, it should become clear that a successful external relationship with the people who use, or could use, libraries depends on there being successful internal relationships between the people who work in them.

As a result of a study carried out for the American Council on Library Resources, Sue Fontaine identified what she termed 'PR Tick/Click'. Library managers considering public relations, says Ms Fontaine, 'identified internal communications as their greatest challenge. For without that internal "tick" generated by open communications and understanding within the library itself . . . there can be no external "click" out there in the community'.[1]

It is outside the scope of this present work to discuss the organization and development of a library communications network. Suffice it to say that ideas, information, and instructions have to be communicated in any library system and that this is achieved, to a greater or lesser extent, through the use of telephones, memos, meetings, notice-boards, staff manuals, reports, and similar commonplace things. Each of these methods of course has its own advantages and disadvantages.

Whatever the medium of communication used, the actual transmission of the message can be impaired by attitudes, emotions, and the other pyschological factors that are present in any organization. Such barriers to effective communication can prevent the internal 'tick' that is, as Ms Fontaine points out, necessary for the external public relations 'click'.

Barriers to communication

This section examines those things that can distort communications as they travel to and from members of a library staff. When talking on the telephone, listening to the radio or watching television, all of us have at some time experienced the effects of interference or noise on the line. Climatic and other disturbances, not being part of the message transmitted, can and do seriously distort it. In interpersonal communication, psychological forces can cause reactions equally strong to those caused by electric currents or climatic conditions. This psychological 'noise' can also result in distorted communication. Sometimes, of course, there may be semantic difficulties but all too often the 'fault' is to be found in the psychological condition of the parties concerned.

Status

One important influence is the relative status of the people involved in a communications encounter. Even in today's more enlightened times, staff are usually less ready to communicate with people far above them in the management hierarchy. The junior assistant will think more than twice before complaining to the chief or even the deputy, while further along the line a branch librarian (say) may withhold information which reflects badly on him or her. You can have the situation where staff are afraid to tell the chief the truth – or at least the whole of it. At the same time, a junior member of staff may also be reluctant to communicate ideas to a superior, reluctant to communicate the kind of creative ideas that can be so important in library public relations and other activities. This attitude can be summed up in the phrase 'Who am I to say?'

Different attitudes

Attitudes can play an important part in interpersonal communications. None of us can take part in the work process without colouring it with our own attitudes. Members of a library staff do not leave their attitudes at the library entrance, they bring them to work with them. The relationship between attitudes and behaviour is a complex one which cannot be explored here, but it is true to say that attitudes can predispose people to perceive and behave in certain ways. Individual attitudes may be the result of self-interest, beliefs, reputation, or the code of the society in which we live and work.

Different feelings

As library managers, it is important that we have the capacity to see and even accept points of view that are different from our own. Each of us tends to see things in terms of our own dominant needs, views, and prejudices. This can lead to very real communications problems. If we are honest, we can all identify certain subjects, ideas, groups, or personalities that set off our emotional trip-wires. In the work situation this can become personalized and individualized, so that a particular member of staff, or for that matter a member of the public, can trigger such a reaction. The stronger these feelings are the less likely the chance of any kind of mutual understanding and communication.

Different values

In libraries, as in life, people are constantly making judgements and evaluations from their own frame of reference. Such judgements may not be mutually acceptable to all concerned. The chief librarian or section head who is deaf to the moods, feelings, and attitudes of his or her staff will probably be unable to judge how staff will react to carefully prepared plans and programmes. When conflict occurs it is often a reflection of the different values held by different sections of the library workforce.

The values of a man who only lives for the job may well appear unreal to the member of staff who likes to spend the maximum amount of time with his family. The sound manager and effective communicator will temper the style of his or her communication so that it is relevant, and at such a level as to be realistic to those on the receiving end. Those readers familiar with hi-fi will know that some tape-recorders have a device called a limiter. The purpose of this is to prevent distortion when recording a signal that is too powerful for the recorder to cope with. Perhaps this type of device should be placed between library staff and some high-powered chiefs, some of whom — to draw another analogy — are transmitting on a wavelength to which few of their staff are 'tuned in'.

Unwillingness

So far, we have assumed that people want to communicate. However, this is not always the case. Harold Pinter is generally thought of as a playwright who is concerned with people's inability to communicate but, in an interesting programme note for *The Birthday Party,* Pinter has indicated that the problem is people's unwillingness to communicate. 'Communication', says Pinter, 'is too alarming. To enter into someone's life is too frightening. To disclose to others the poverty within us is too fearsome a possibility.' Very often the 'flow of speech is a desperate rearguard attempt to keep ourselves to ourselves'.[2] The psychologists among my readers will recognise in this type of behaviour the operation of defence mechanisms.

One can observe these defences being erected in a number of communication situations. For example, consider the case of a library manager discussing a report or event with a subordinate. The manager will pick and pick again on one detail and the discussion will revolve around this. The manager will rationalize such behaviour as efficiency and shrewdness, but what is really happening? By concentrating on a minor aspect of the topic, the manager is building a defence against communicating (and perhaps taking a decision) on the major issue.

We should also consider the effect of this behaviour on the person on the receiving end. The member of staff concerned is in a kind of bibliographical dock and, while it may be the function of Rumpole of the Bailey or Petrocelli to destroy a case on a point of detail, it is not an appropriate role for a library manager. When dealing with staff, it is important to encourage them to make the best contribution that they can. This is not going to be achieved by constant 'nit picking' which can very quickly destroy a subordinate's confidence.

Understanding people

Managers need to understand the hopes, fears, and aspirations of their staff and this means listening to them. Perhaps the greatest barrier to personal communication is an inability to listen intelligently and sympathetically to another person. To do this you must put yourself in the other person's place, you must analyze and be sensitive to that person's moods, wants, and feelings.

A democratic participative style of management should make it easier for staff to communicate upwards. However, all too often in libraries one sees pseudo-democratic management in which the structure may allow for participation but the chief holds on to a central position in any discussion. He or she keeps the reins of power and does not really let the group interfere with his or her method of working. This type of behaviour has a detrimental effect on human relations and staff public relations.

Integrating

The good manager aims to make each member of staff feel important and that he or she is contributing to the total library picture. Each assistant, each porter, should be made to feel that he or she matters. The management should demonstrate that it recognizes the individual worth of each member of staff.

To junior assistants and sometimes even to those somewhat higher in the hierarchy, top management can appear detached and impersonal. Their everyday work in the library seems to be controlled by impersonal forces and they begin to feel rather like the assembly-line worker in *Modern Times*. A chief who makes time to visit staff in branches and out-of-the-way departments can do much to alleviate this problem.

It is essential to integrate the individual staff member into the library organization. In some circumstances this may mean altering the management structure. As Argyris writes, 'it involves a modification of the pyramid structure of command which centralizes control at the top. Ways must be found to increase autonomy and control down through the organization'.[3]

Discussing

Another way to help counter feelings of detachment is for a senior member of the library management to discuss with staff their hopes, fears, and career prospects. A number of commercial organizations have introduced formal provision for what are called appraisal and development interviews'. This is perhaps a development that could be usefully copied by library organizations.[4] Too often, the first indication that someone is unhappy in his or her job comes with a request for a reference.

Keeping staff informed

Staff should always be kept informed of changes that will concern them and their working lives. Librarians, of all people, should realize that information is a human need. The communication of information to staff is not just desirable, it is essential. Staff should be told well in advance about matters that will affect them, explanations should be given where appropriate, and the fullest possible information relayed. There are times when management cannot tell all but each manager should look very carefully at the reasons for withholding information and should make sure that it is not merely a way of retaining personal knowledge and power.

Above all, one should communicate honestly. A library can have the best of all possible communications networks but it will fail unless staff believe in the honesty of the message. Where there is distrust, even the most straightforward memo or report will be critically examined for hidden meanings. If a library management fails to communicate with its staff, it is creating the conditions in which the grapevine will grow and flourish. The grapevine fills the vacuum left by a lack of information and it is a plant that grows strong on gossip and rumour.

Performance and perception

The effective communication of information makes staff more aware of their total working environment. This helps human relations and improves staff morale and performance. It is staff performance above all that affects people's perception of the library and the service it offers. Moreover it is the performance of the more junior members of staff that impinges on most users. The clerk behind the counter can make or mar the library service in the eyes of the public.

If we think of ourselves as users of services, then all of us can recall encounters in shops, banks, or railway stations that have coloured our views of those services. In the same way, the reception that a client receives can affect his or her view of the public library service. Library managers must train staff so that they attend to the public in a pleasant, helpful, and friendly way. Senior staff should cultivate this attitude. All staff should remember that the library to a large extent depends on its clients. Readers' enquiries, however trivial they may appear, should not be regarded or treated as interruptions to work — they are the work.

Non-verbal behaviour

The first encounter of a close kind that a person has with a library service can shape his or her attitudes towards that service in the future. Many years ago, a library staff went on strike because a committee member accused them of not smiling. Whatever the rights or wrongs of that particular case, the council member was correct to emphasize the importance of smiling and other non-verbal behaviour.

The whole topic of non-verbal communication has been covered by Michael Argyle,[5] Desmond Morris,[6] and others, and it is not intended to go into detail in the present work, though much remains to be done in examining non-verbal behaviour in the library context. For our present purposes, it is sufficient to consider very briefly the role of non-verbal communication (NVC) in social interaction.

When dealing with people, we make use of both verbal and non-verbal communication, and often use a combination of both. In strict linguistic terms, the difference between verbal and non-verbal communication is between communications that make use of *words* and those that do not. As Lyons[7] has written, a serious problem in discussing the subject 'is the inconsistency and imprecision with which the distinction between "verbal" and "non-verbal" has been drawn'. However, this 'inconsistency' may be inherent in the nature of the subject. There are times, for instance, when there is a potential overlap between the roles of VC and NVC in social interaction. Furthermore, it would be wrong to suggest that VC and NVC are always carrying out independent functions.

Communicating attitudes

Non-verbal communication plays a significant part in establishing social relationships. Interpersonal attitudes are communicated by means of posture, facial expression, and appearance. Posture, for instance, can indicate an inferior/superior relationship, while facial expression can show liking or dislike. Verbal communication can also, of course, be used to establish rapport between people. What Sapir[8] has described as the 'caressing or re-assuring quality of speech' can be seen in the 'small talk' that manifests itself in many social situations, including those that take place across a library counter.

Facial expression often modifies what a person is saying or doing, showing whether it is supposed to be serious, funny, important, friendly, or otherwise. One notes how television newsreaders adopt a suitable expression for reading reports of tragedies, or deaths of the famous. In a library, a member of staff's facial reaction to a reader or an enquiry can convey all kinds of messages to the client.

Non-verbal communication plays a significant role in self-presentation. That is how a person wishes to be seen in terms of (say) status. The self can be presented through such things as appearance, aspects of speech, or posture. Appearance, says Argyle,[9] is used to signal attitudes towards other people.

Dress

Today, dress is in itself a main dimension of appearance. In the library, fashionably dressed staff can be a public relations asset. There is certainly no need to enforce the dress rules of a bygone age. Indeed, in some circumstances too formal a style of dress may form a barrier between a librarian and a prospective client. Dress may be interpreted as an indication of class and this can certainly affect a social encounter. For example, in an interesting experiment carried out for the Open University[10] an actor drew different responses to his request for information depending on his apparent social class as indicated by different styles of dress. One should add that this experiment did not involve librarians but, nevertheless, its results are of some significance to them.

Personal contact

Communicating with library clients, like most social encounters, involves a complex interaction of verbal and non-verbal signals. Nods, grunts — the giving and receiving of verbal and non-verbal 'rewards' — are important for the synchronization of utterances. It has been said that 'we speak with our vocal organs but converse . . . with our whole body'.[11] The role of kinesics (bodily movements) in gaining and holding a person's attention, signalling attentiveness and sustaining a conversation has been ably demonstrated by those involved with the practice of social skills therapy.

A little thought will reveal that interpersonal skills can play an important part in public relations in the practical library work context. Any librarian responsible for a direct service to the public should be aware of the importance of personal contact with users.

Counter staff should be encouraged, through training, to meet and greet clients. A friendly smile and a word of greeting can only help a person feel more welcome and more at ease. Experiments carried out in some American libraries have shown that clients who are lightly touched on the hand by counter assistants have a more favourable view of the library than those who are not.[12]

It is an interesting sidelight on the introduction of computer charging systems that many counter staff, used to Brown charging, miss the personal contact that that system allowed. While long conversations are an obvious waste of staff time, a few words about the weather or even books do not come amiss!

Understanding the client

At all times, staff should be encouraged to attend and assist library users. A client's request for help should be given top priority. Above all, staff should avoid becoming animated signposts, simply pointing users in the direction of shelves or catalogues. 'It's over there' is a phrase that should be banned from all library enquiry desks. As we have seen above, a superior attitude can very easily be communicated to the client by non-verbal means. Staff should make an effort to avoid appearing condescending when faced with a 'trivial' request. It may seem unimportant to the staff but is likely to be important to the reader. It is not the function of library staff — nor should it be — to stand in judgement over readers' tastes.

If people who make a considerable psychological investment in asking a question are made to feel that their requests are a waste of time, they may not ask for help again. If they are unable to find their way round the library, they may simply leave it. A library is a familiar place for a librarian, but for many people it can be more than a little frightening. Staff should, therefore, 'study' their clients so as to be able to appreciate their problems. Knowing the clients in order to satisfy their needs should be the aim of the staff of any service institution. In terms of public relations there is no better publicity than the recommendation of a satisfied client.

Complaints

Even in a library where the management pays close attention to interpersonal skills, training, and other matters mentioned above, there will always be some disgruntled clients. What is a librarian or library assistant to do when faced with an angry borrower? The circumstances surrounding any particular case will, of course, have to be taken into account, but there are some general lines of action which it can sometimes be helpful to adopt. At least try the following:

1. Listen to the client's side of the story. This will help you to find out what the 'problem' is.
2. Allow clients to ventilate their anger.
3. Do not argue. This will only antagonize the client further.
4. As the client's anger subsides, look for points of agreement on the issue in question.
5. Try to keep, as far as possible, a friendly atmosphere.
6. If the client is justifiably annoyed and something has gone wrong, put the matter right as quickly as possible. To delay will only make matters worse.
7. If all this does not work refer the matter to a more senior member of staff. He or she will probably have to repeat the sequence.

There may be some difficult clients who insist on taking the matter further and they should be invited to write to, or make an appointment to see, the chief librarian or head of department. In such circumstances, the chief or department head should be told of the complaint and appraised of the circumstances surrounding it.

Complaints received by a library should be taken seriously and used constructively. They are, after all, a manifestation of a client's dissatisfaction with the service. What is more, a complaint from just one client may be an indication of a more widespread lack of satisfaction. Public libraries might usefully consider following the procedures of some airlines and hotel chains and actually solicit comments and suggestions from users on the range and quality of services offered. This could be achieved by having forms on the checkout counter inviting users to make their feelings known. A general invitation might read: 'We like to know that our service gives satisfaction. If you have any cause for complaint please let us know so we can take steps to put things right. We should also be encouraged to hear of any particular reason you have to be especially pleased with the range and quality of our services.'

This type of exercise would help communicate clients' impressions of the service to the library management.

Telephone technique

A client's impression of a library service may be gained through the telephone and, as with personal contact, first impressions are important. The telephone is a major point of contact between a library and its publics. It is the voice of the library and all staff should be made fully aware of the importance of developing good telephone technique. The telephone should be answered promptly and callers should be made to feel that their call is welcome. Staff should be trained to answer the phone with a phrase such as, 'Good morning, this is Biblioville Public Library, can I help you?' A few words before the library identification are useful so as to enable a caller to adjust to any unfamiliar accent.

Public relations can be seriously damaged by poor telephone techniques. 'Lost' telephone calls, mishandled enquiries, and long waits between transfers do not help promote a favourable view of the library. During telephone conversations, non-verbal cues cannot be received by the person on the end of the line but verbal cues, such as 'I see', can be used to encourage the client.

Large library systems can afford to employ trained telephonists and there is no doubt that a good professional in this field, as in others, is an asset. However, all staff have to use the telephone and they should make sure that their callers receive quick, clear, efficient, and effective attention. The telephone is an important medium of communication and it is worth ringing round the various service points in your own system to check just what the library's voice sounds like. If it sounds really bad, you might ask the Post Office to arrange a training session for your staff. This they will sometimes do free of charge.

There are other public relations functions that the telephone can perform. For example, Ansafone services can be used to record renewals and enquiries out of library hours. In addition, the telephone service can be used to disseminate children's bedtime stories, poetry readings, and the like.

As we indicated in the first chapter, public relations means establishing a mutual understanding between an organization and its publics. At no time is this more important than when dealing directly with people, be they staff or public. Good, continuous communication is a way of avoiding misunderstandings which can seriously damage a library's internal and external public relations. The success or failure of such communication depends to a large extent on the attitude of management. The ability to keep communication channels clear is one of the most important and potentially productive skills that a library manager can possess.

NOTES AND REFERENCES

1. Fontaine, S *Report to the Council on Library Resources. Public Relations in Public Libraries*, 1975.
2. Pinter, H, Programme note for *The Birthday Party* as performed by The Royal Shakespeare Company at the Aldwych Theatre, 1964.
3. Argyris, C *Integrating the individual and the organisation*, Wiley, 1964.
4. The British Library Lending Division has recently introduced such interviews for its staff.
5. See for example:
   Argyle, M *Social interaction*, Methuen, 1969.
   Argyle, M *Bodily communication*, Methuen, 1975.
   Argyle, M & Trower, P *Person to person, ways of communicating*, Harper & Row, 1979.
6. Morris, D *Manwatching*, Cape, 1977.
7. Lyons, J 'Human language' in Hinde, RA (ed.) *Non verbal communication*, Cambridge University Press, 1972.
8. Sapir, E 'Language' *in* Thompson, K & Tunstall, J *Sociological Perspectives*, Penguin, 1971.
9. Argyle, M *Bodily communication*, Methuen, 1975.
10. See: Sissons, M 'The psychology of social class' in *Money Wealth and Class* (Understanding Society. Units 14–18), Open University Press, 1971.
11. Abercrombie, K 'Paralanguage' in *Br. J. Dis Comm* 3(1) April 1968.
12. These experiments were reported in the BBC 2 *Horizon* programme first televised on 5 November 1979.

Chapter 11
Community Public Relations

It is a professional cliché to state that librarians should know their communities. However, like a good many clichés, it contains more than a little truth. A knowledge of local communities is an essential pre-requisite if a public library is going to develop and maintain an effective public relations programme. No two communities are the same and what might be a sound promotional idea in one area may not work in another.

Community appreciation of a library service is of considerable practical value. Whether, as in some parts of the United States, the library has to appeal directly to the public for budget support or, as in Great Britain, receives finance as part of a local authority, a public library needs to enlist the interest and support of groups within the local community. In addition to this fiscal dimension, positive community attitudes towards a library service can help the library organization when seeking to appoint staff in competition with other local agencies.

Moreover, as 'The Hillingdon Report'[1] demonstrated, community attitudes can be a very real barrier to library effectiveness as can people's perception of library services. The atmosphere of libraries was frequently mentioned unfavourably in the Hillingdon study:

'When I think of a library, I see one thing in front of my eyes, and that's SILENCE'.
'My wife works in a morgue, libraries are just like that. You can see that council stigma on them (librarians) as soon as you walk in.'
'Everybody looks at a library as being dead.'
'The atmosphere is not church-like — it's even worse'.

All this is evidence that much public relations work remains to be done.

One American librarian has said that some libraries need 'to embark on a program to change the perception of a vast number . . . in the community who look upon the public library only as an institution which provides reading material for children and lovers of books'.[2]

The community perception of a library service may be quite different from that of the professional librarians who work for it. One of the reasons for this is that people who live and work in a community very often have a different view of a community than those who simply work in it. Alex Glasgow[3] has written a pointed little song about the damaging effects of architects and planners who design inner-city environments having 'saved themselves a cottage in the hills'. It would perhaps be unrealistic to expect every librarian to live in the area she or he serves but we should nevertheless heed Glasgow's warning of the dangers of providing a service for a community while living apart from it.

Know the community

Librarians must be aware of the main features of the community they serve. There is a need to build up a profile of the community, so that services and promotional activities can be developed in tune with the needs and aspirations of individuals and groups within the community. This means considering factors such as the age, race, and social structure of the population, cultural traditions, land usage, housing and transport patterns.

There are various recorded sources of information about any community that the librarian should consult. For example, census figures, local government data, and other statistical records. The history of a community can often help to explain current circumstances and this will be found in local newspapers, parish histories, files of local clubs and organizations, town guides, directories and handbooks. Community profiling is a topic in its own right and the reader is referred to some useful publications at the end of this chapter.[4]

Although it is used here for convenience, I am aware that 'community' is an overworked word. There are in fact around one hundred definitions of the word. One writer has observed: 'In the loose application of the term the word community has become a maid of all work whose use should be banished completely from everyday parlance, since it has created nothing but confusion'.[5]

Be that as it may, we have no alternative but to use the word and for the purposes of this book I will follow Frankenberg who says: 'community implies having something in common'.[6] This common factor may be a geographical location, the membership of a club or institution, race, age, sex, or a common interest in beekeeping, cricket or hang-gliding. There are many such communities in the geographical area served by the average public library and each of these has its own communications network. As part of her or his public relations activities the librarian should try to 'plug in' to these networks.

Participation

There are many ways in which librarians and their staff can participate in the life of the community. Local clubs and organizations provide library staff with very real opportunities to involve themselves in local affairs. Staff should be encouraged in their work with and for such bodies. The community's view of the library service may at times depend on what staff do outside normal working hours. There are also other obvious community communications networks, such as the local press and broadcasting, and these are discussed elsewhere. In addition, the church, pub or club are also very often significant disseminators of community information and ideas.

A librarian should also seek to identify and contact the 'leaders' of the local community. These are the people whose help should be enlisted to assist in establishing a favourable attitude to the library service. Fellow local government officers, church leaders, school teachers, bank managers, trade union officials, youth workers, and so on all have specialized knowledge of a neighbourhood and contact with them will help to increase the librarian's knowledge of the local community and its power structures.

The role of action groups

The traditional local power structures are, in many areas, now being changed by the appearance of new and important grass roots organizations that seek to influence local authority decisions. Rotary Clubs, Chambers of Commerce, and similar bodies have long been recognized by local government officers and elected members as important pressure groups. Now, community action groups are seeking to extend the range of influence so as to include the poorer and less articulate sections of the community. Public librarians should welcome this development because it provides yet another channel through which the library's message can be transmitted. Equally important, it is a channel through which the needs of an important, but often neglected, section of the local population can be articulated.

When making contact with groups of this kind, the librarian should make the most of the opportunity provided to explain the vital role the library can play in the community. By so doing, she or he can win and hold the support of this section of the public. Community action groups are often suspicious of local government, so the librarian should not use the stilted official approach of the town hall, but present the library service so that it is seen to be relevant to the hopes and aspirations of the people concerned.

Reaching the non-user

In 1978, following the publication of *Libraries are ours*,[7] an informal meeting was held in Glasgow involving community groups, librarians, library users, and others concerned with the dissemination of information. One of the things to emerge from this meeting was proof that an involved community will support its library service. The question remains of how to reach the uninvolved, in particular those in the more deprived areas, where there is no tradition of library use.

Though there are no easy answers to this question, some solutions may be found in other chapters dealing with publications, displays, and staff attitudes. The task, as always, is to make the library relevant to community needs and to demonstrate that

Library user councils

Those responsible for providing library services must listen to the community. One of the most important aspects of community public relations is the feedback it can provide of local attitudes, needs, and demands. It has been suggested that Library User Councils might be a way of providing such feedback. William Murison has said that such groups 'could be a most useful channel for conveying complaints and suggestions which would help librarians', though he warns that they could also be 'a time-consuming pain in the neck'.[8]

Similar groups have been set up by BBC local radio stations. These are advisory bodies of volunteers who live in a station's broadcasting area. Local Radio Councils, as they are known, are not intended as simply supporters' clubs for the station but as bodies of well-informed local people who, in various ways, represent community views to the radio station and the radio station to the community.

Friends

In the United States, Friends' groups have for many years provided a link between libraries and the publics they serve. There have also been some recent experiments with such groups in Great Britain, notably in Devon and Somerset. Friends' groups were first formed in the USA to support academic libraries, the first public library group being formed in 1922. Since that time, hundreds of such groups have been established and many of these have achieved a great deal.

Fund-raising

One of the major functions of American Friends' groups has been fund-raising. This has been achieved through such activities as 'buy a brick' campaigns, book and record sales, gift shops, and celebrity events. Friends also play an important part in mobilizing public support when a library is faced with a direct public vote on its budget. British libraries do not have to go directly to the public for their monies to be approved but the quite sophisticated lobbying techniques developed by some American Friends groups could well be of use if applied in the United Kingdom. These will be discussed in greater detail in Chapter 12 but for the moment I will concentrate on Friends' groups as a part of community involvement.

Promoting the library

In terms of public relations, Friends' can do much to increase the visibility of the library in the community. At the same time, they can communicate community needs to the library's administration. Friends' groups are almost always independent of the library's formal organization but their programmes and activities are generally planned in consultation with the library's management.

In the United States, I was able to spend some time with the Secretary of the Friends' group associated with the Free Library of Philadelphia. This is a flourishing group and one that has been particularly active in community public relations. For example, in April 1978 it organized a 'Neighbourhood Leadership Night' which was a 'special program for influential citizen leaders and community organizers'. In a two-hour programme, community leaders were presented with a slide show demonstrating how the library could contribute to 'the social and material well-being of your neighbourhood'. In addition, representatives of community organizations were invited to ask 'what can the Free Library do for us?' This was followed by a response from the Director of the Library and the President of the Friends' group. One of the community organizations was the Community Service Center for the

Friends: For $200 Cincinnati residents can buy part of 'a memorial wall in which will be placed "signature bricks" of individuals and business firms who wish to have a permanent memorial in their name'. On the right membership identifications from Jackson County and West Virginia Libraries.

Deaf, so the library responded to their particular needs by providing an interpreter for deaf members of the audience.

Friends' groups in themselves seek to represent, and be representative of, their local community. They tend, therefore, to have a range of membership categories. These are based on an annual financial contribution. There are, for example, six grades for the Philadelphia group: (1978 figures)

> Non-voting $5–14 subscription
> Sustaining $15–99
> Sponsor $100–249
> Patron $250+
> Full-time student (non-voting) $2
> Senior Citizen $2

The higher grades ($100–250+) are intended for 'businesses, civic groups, and foundations who wish to join on something beyond the individual level'.[9] The Sustaining members, who form the largest group of membership, receive a number of privileges, such as discounted admission to library events.

The annual operating budget of the Philadelphia group is estimated at around $40,000 and it employs a number of staff, including a full-time executive director and secretary. Like many such groups it operates out of an office in the library itself.

PR Activities

Friends' groups often undertake their own public relations activities and one or two librarians that I spoke to in the United States expressed the view that duplication of PR effort could sometimes be a problem. The range of these activities is wide and includes such things as newsletters, press releases, galas, tape-slide presentations, workshops, 'touch the author' sessions, library tours, and radio and television exposure.

'The Philadelphia's Friends' greatest coup was in securing a substantial segment on the Mike Douglas show (a popular late-night talk and entertainment show) which mentioned the Friends and showed extensive footage of the Central Library . . . How was it done? By the simple expedient of having Princess Grace of

Monaco doing the commentary, in connection with the donation of her uncle George Kelly's papers to the library's theater collection'.[10] Such blockbusting activities are rare but many Friends groups arrange their own community programmes and events.

Informing the community

Friends' groups also play a vital part in spreading the library word through the local media, thus helping to keep the community informed about its library and the facilities it offers. The techniques described elsewhere in this work can all be used to this end. Library publications, for example, should be distributed in pubs, doctors' waiting-rooms, and other community buildings. Displays can and should be mounted in stores, factories, and the like. The library service should make itself known by taking part in county shows, neighbourhood fairs, and street festivals.

Individuals and groups in the community can contribute to the library's publications programme, by being invited to submit reviews of new books and records acquired by the library. Recently, in the United States at least, community cookery books have proved to be very popular library publications. Plainedge Public Library, for example, published *Plainedge Potpourri*[11] which, in addition to being a collection of recipes supplied by members of the community, was a potpourri of articles and photographs reflecting the history of Plainedge.

Such activities help to communicate the library's message to the general public, but efforts should also be made to reach individual groups in a community, in particular, to reach those who feel that library services are not for them. The problem is to change these people's perception of the library service and what it can offer.

Joseph Eisner, the director at Plainedge, believes that direct mail can be an effective way of doing this. His library has started publishing special-interest newsletters. These are mailed to people known to be interested in the topic covered. In addition to the subject information contained in the text, these newsletters sometimes contain lists of appropriate material available at the library. Eisner is realistic about the usefulness of these. He says, 'the infrequent or non-library-user is less likely to be motivated to come to the library to obtain these materials. Information in hand would appear to be more effective'.[12]

Ethnic minorities

Special efforts should be made to reach the ethnic minorities present within many public library communities. The need for publicity in appropriate languages has already been stressed elsewhere, but ethnic groups should also be approached through their own community associations and organizations. Public libraries should also promote events of special relevance to members of ethnic communities. Such activities might include black writers' exhibitions, musical evenings, or film shows. It is important that such functions are not perceived as being imposed on a community and the librarian should consult and cooperate with representatives of the groups concerned. Although their role is obviously wider than just that of public relations, the appointment of community liaison officers in Leicestershire, Westminster and elsewhere is a welcome development and one that should be copied by other public library authorities.

Schoolchildren

There is another group that requires special attention. That is schoolchildren. Though we might argue about the degree, there can be little doubt that for many people what they learn at school has a lasting effect on their future actions, attitudes, and aspirations. It is, therefore, particularly important to make children aware of the value and relevance of public library services. This, of course, also means making teachers aware of the public library's potential so that they can encourage pupils to use it.

Many teachers are now in fact telling their students about the use and importance of community information, and this should expand the potential part that the public library can play in the lives of young people. The British Library, through its 'Need to Know'[13] project, based at South Hackney School in London, recently examined methods of promoting such services within the framework of a school instruction programme.

School visits to libraries are a traditional method of introducing children to public library facilities. Some have criticized this activity on the basis that it links the library too closely to the formal education system. This, it is argued, may actually put off those children who do not like, or do not succeed at school. There is no one right or wrong answer to this problem and it would be quite incorrect to generalize. In deciding the policy to be followed, the individual librarian must be sensitive to the problems and/or opportunities presented by his or her own locality.

The public library should attempt to build up goodwill among all sections of its community. Some areas have been highlighted in this chapter and others, such as the business community, elsewhere. Relations with these various communities should be fostered and carefully nurtured, not only to increase the community's use of the library service, but also to ensure its support for that service when economic times are hard.

NOTES AND REFERENCES

1   Totterdell, B & Bird, J *The effective library* (Report of the Hillingdon Project on Public Library Effectiveness) ed. M Redfern, Library Association, 1976.
2   Eisner, J 'Marketing for public libraries'. A speech delivered to the Rockland County Public Library Association on 14 June 1978.
3   Glasgow, A 'The Mary Baker City Mix' on *Songs of Alex Glasgow Two*, MWM Records, 1009.
4   A number of libraries have produced variations on the community profiling theme. For example:
    Bedfordshire County Library, *Houghton Regis: A study of the library in its community,* Bedfordshire County Library, 1974.
    Bedfordshire County Library, *Leighton Buzzard: a community profile . . . in three parts, dated May 1975, February 1976 and June 1976,* Bedfordshire County Library, 1976.
    Cheshire Libraries and Museums, *Runcorn District Library Market Research Study,* 1978.
    Cumbria County Library, 'The Ambleside library survey', July 1975, (unpublished).
    Suffolk County Library, *Word pictures of service points,* 1979.

There is also a useful introduction to profiling: Jordan, P & Walley, E *Learning about the community,* School of Librarianship, Leeds Polytechnic, 1977.
5   Konig, R *The community,* trans. Edward Fitzgerald, Routledge & Kegan Paul Ltd, 1968.
6   Frankenberg, R *Communities in Britain,* Penguin, 1970.
7   Darcy, B & Ohri, A *Libraries are ours,* Community Projects Foundation, 1978.
8   Murison, W J 'Users – pain or profit?' Letter in *Lib. Ass. Rec.* 80(11), November 1978.
    The British Library has now published a report by Mr Murison on Users' Consultative Councils, (see bibliography p199). In addition, following consultations with him, the National Consumer Council is developing a 'library checklist' for use by groups and individuals wishing to assess the service offered by their public library.
9   From a publicity leaflet produced by the Friends of the Free Library of Philadelphia.
10 Pennell, H B and others *Find out who your friends are,* The Friends of the Free Library of Philadelphia Inc., 1978.
11 *Plainedge potpourri,* Plainedge Public Library, 1976.
12 Eisner, J 'Marketing for Public Libraries'. ibid
13 *The Need to Know: teaching the importance of information,* final report for the period January 1978 – March 1979 (BLR & D report 5511), British Library, 1979.

Chapter 12
Councillors, Councils and Committees

An essential function of library public relations is to influence favourably those people who take decisions about the public library service. It is a fact of library life that public libraries need the support of politicians at both national and local level. The question of the library profession's relationship with national government will be discussed in Chapter 15. This section deals with the relationships between the local librarian, the local legislators, and the local community.

Politicians are responsive to local public opinion. The librarian who works with the local community and gains its support will have public opinion on his or her side. For this to happen, the library service must be willing to respond to the needs of the local people. With some notable exceptions, the response of public libraries to the needs of community groups has been disappointing. When local politicians cut a library's budget, librarians sometimes complain at the lack of vocal public support for their cause. Perhaps more support would be forthcoming if more ordinary working people felt their local library to be relevant to their own everyday needs, hopes, and aspirations.

Political action

Librarians can persuade politicians by working through the people. This is the theme taken up in a *Budget Action Handbook* issued to the staff of the New York Public Library. This has been compiled 'to serve as a guide for working with citizen support groups, for implementing budget and political action'.

Although, as explained earlier, the American financial and political arrangements are different from those operating in Britain, it is useful to consider some of the lobbying techniques of American

Friends' and library support groups. There is some evidence of groups of this kind being established in Britain and some of the American techniques could well be adapted for use in the British political context.

These techniques include letter-writing campaigns in which a standard format is used but each writer adds an individual note of his or her personal requirements. A sample letter for a budget campaign might read as follows:

```
The Honourable          _____
Councilmember           _____
Address                 _____


Dear Councilmember      _____:


The Mayor's proposed 1978-79 Expense Budget not only fails to bring
The          Public Library closer to meeting minimum state standards
regarding hours of service, but calls for the elimination of 17
positions. I urge you to work for the rescindment of the staffing
cuts, and the addition of personnel to bring the Library closer to
the state standards. Right now, almost 90% of the Library's branches
are below the minimum state standards.

Library service is vital to my community (important to me) because ...

     (Here writer gives own reasons such as:

     Cannot afford double car fares to go to branch further away;
     Needs Saturday service;
     Use by children, seniors, handicapped, etc.;
     Student use;
     No branch nearby, need continued bookmobile service;
     Need film library in Borough;
     Spanish materials;
     Use of meeting rooms for community meetings;
     Free programs;
     High school equivalency, vocational materials, etc.)

I expect you to work vigorously to ensure that The       Public
Library receives a priority status for funds in the 1978-79 Expense
Budget, and that library funding be increased and maintained in the
future.

                                    Very truly yours,




                                    Name and Address
```

Sample letter, City Expense Budget Campaign

Telephone campaigns have also been used with some success, and many groups have used luncheons, dinners or banquets 'to get various powerful political leaders to show support for the library, and to show others who the library supporters were'.[1]

In West Virginia, the library has run three very successful legislative campaigns: the library 'Pin Pal' Campaign, the library Pie Campaign, and the library Tie Campaign. The Pin Pal Campaign included the presentation of pins, with an accompanying explanation, to legislators and a library pin pal Dinner. The library Pie Campaign, with the slogan 'Library pie requires State dough', also involved food. Legislators were presented with a newly baked pie and a recipe for 'original West Virginia Library Pie'. The 'cooking instructions' concluded: 'To complete the library pie State dough is needed to hold it together'. As part of the library Tie Campaign all legislators were presented with a library tie or scarf. There was also the inevitable dinner and slogan: 'Tie one on for the library'.

All this may seem far removed from the world of British local government and no doubt the nature of such campaigns is shaped by the American economic and cultural context. However, they do demonstrate public relations flair and an immense sense of fun — two ingredients that could surely be added to our own system of local government.

Members and officers

One of the key relationships in British local government is that between the chief officer and the chairperson of the responsible committee. With the advent of corporate management and multi-purpose departments and committees, many chief librarians ceased to be chief officers. A number within the public library profession feel that this has made access to the chairperson much more difficult. As Corbett writes: 'From the Chief Librarian's point of view one of the less agreeable results of a directorate may be his diminished contact with the chairman of the committee and other members of the Council, as well as with his opposite numbers in the Town Hall'.[2]

The same theme was taken up in a recent INLOGOV report

which stated: 'In a number of authorities it is possible to speak of the various chief officers competing with each other before the committee, attempting to build up good relations with the Chairman to get his ear'.[3]

It is vital for the chief librarian to have the chairperson's ear, because it is the chairperson who will put the library's case in council and, perhaps even more important, at the meetings of the majority party group. It is crucial to keep the chairperson fully briefed. In most local authorities there will be some kind of official briefing or 'call over' before committees but the chairperson should be fully informed at all times. The librarian must continually provide the politician with notes and information about the service, so that he or she can talk to people in an informed way. The librarian and chairperson should meet on an informal basis between committees. In some authorities, the chairperson is invited to attend meetings of the departmental management team.

As indicated in an earlier chapter, the chairperson may be expected to write, or at least sign, replies to letters in the press. It is also reasonable to ask him or her to sign letters of thanks for donations, and perhaps also letters of congratulation to staff graduating from library school.

In his highly readable, if somewhat idiosyncratic, war-time publication *The librarian and his committee,* the late E A Savage wrote: 'The relations of committeemen with the librarian are easier if every member knows how the library functions behind the scenes'. This is equally true today and the librarian should arrange for relevant committee members to tour the branches and departments at least once a year. Such an event should be used, not only as an opportunity to show off new equipment and services, but also as a chance to explain and demonstrate operational and other difficulties. New members of the council too can usefully be invited to visit and use the library service.

The existence of an effective local government information service for members and officers can also help councillor/librarian relationships and the holding of ward 'surgeries' in branch libraries brings councillors and constituents into contact with the library service.

Life is easier for a librarian if councillors are receptive to her or

LEGISLATIVE TIPS FROM THE WEST VIRGINIA LIBRARY COMMISSION

The best way to give tips on getting legislative funding is to show off elements of two campaigns which did the financial trick for us. Both were a lot of fun - in fact, the "fun" aspect was like "a spoonful fo sugar to make the medicine go down." Please address any inquiries for further information to: Frederic J. Glazer, Director; West Virginia Library Commission; Science and Cultural Center; Charleston, WV 25305

LEGISLATIVE CAMPAIGN: "LIBRARY PIE REQUIRES STATE DOUGH"

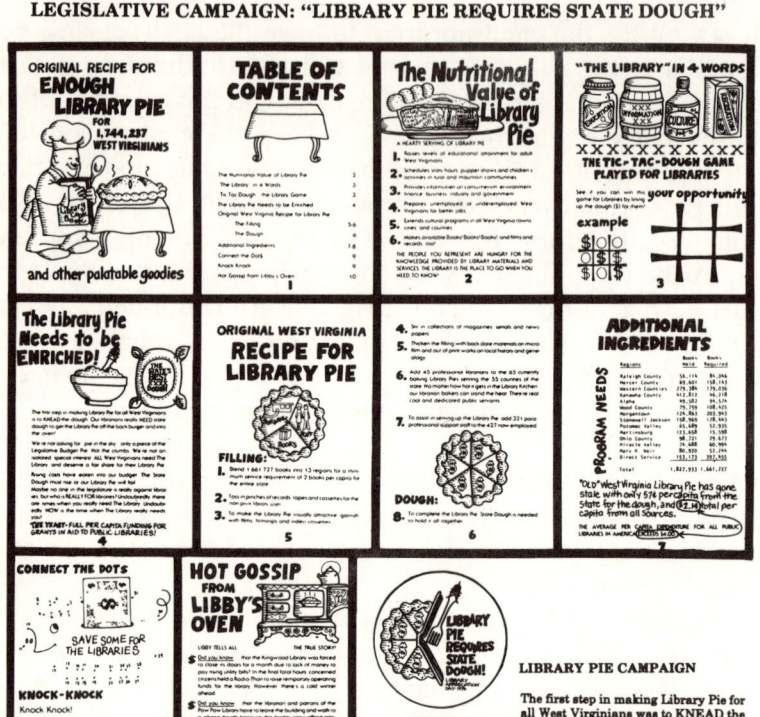

BOOKLET EXCERPTS

BUTTON

PIE PLATE

LIBRARY PIE CAMPAIGN

The first step in making Library Pie for all West Virginians was to KNEAD the dough. Library supporters from all over the state unanimously expressed the fact that libraries NEED the "state dough" to get our pie off the back burner and into the oven. "Library Pie" came into its full flavor and meaning when it was presented to each Legislator, either at the Capitol or at "Library Appreciation Day" celebrations held throughout the State. Each pie was baked in a dish with a message and accompanied by "the facts", tastefully presented in a Recipe Book.

LEGISLATIVE CAMPAIGN: "TIE ONE ON FOR THE LIBRARY"

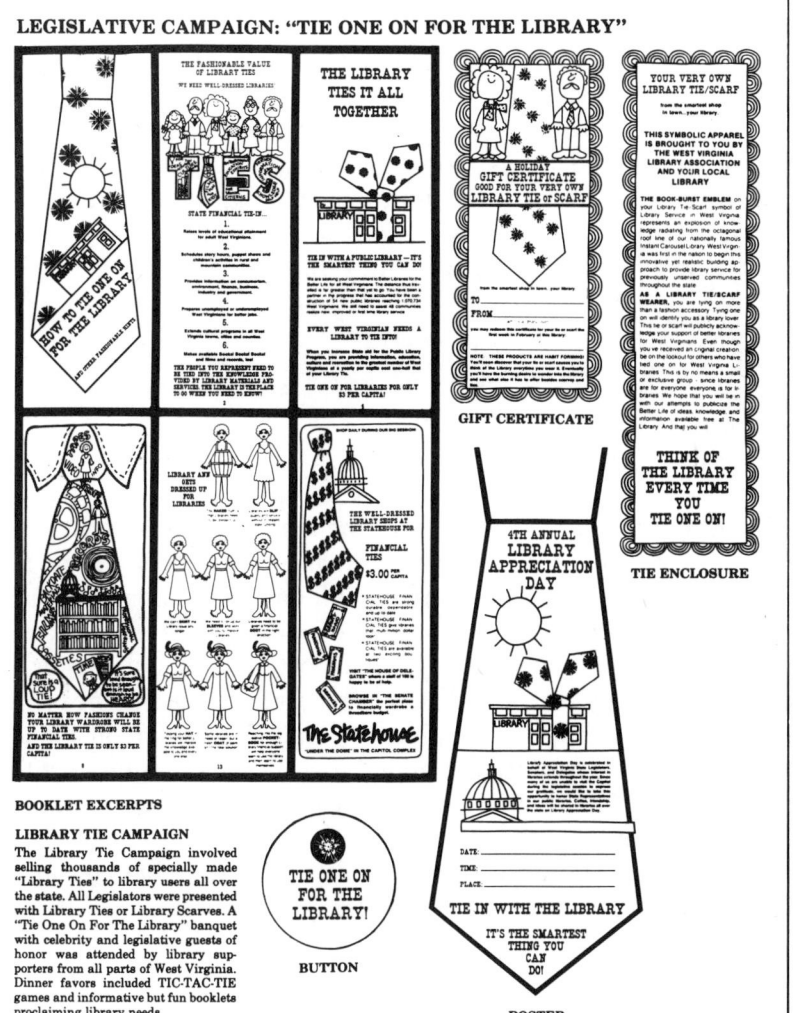

GIFT CERTIFICATE

TIE ENCLOSURE

BUTTON

POSTER

BOOKLET EXCERPTS

LIBRARY TIE CAMPAIGN

The Library Tie Campaign involved selling thousands of specially made "Library Ties" to library users all over the state. All Legislators were presented with Library Ties or Library Scarves. A "Tie One On For The Library" banquet with celebrity and legislative guests of honor was attended by library supporters from all parts of West Virginia. Dinner favors included TIC-TAC-TIE games and informative but fun booklets proclaiming library needs.

his ideas. It helps to know members and their interests and it pays to keep in touch with their activities by following their careers via the local press and radio. Staff should be aware of council members who use their particular branch. In some authorities, working groups of all levels of staff and council members have proved productive. In the words of one of my American friends, the aim is 'to create the miracle of the library-aware legislator'. Savage may not have used those precise words but he would have certainly agreed with the sentiment that they express.

Committees

The committee lies at the heart of the local government decision-making process. There are many criticisms of the committee system and any librarian who, after a full day's work, has had to sit through three or four hours of low-level discussion on matters of little importance, will probably share most of them. One writer has observed: 'Many a "good idea" has emerged at the other end of a committee operation as a kind of "bad dream" mangled and amputated in its essentials, padded together with fantasies into a monster that finally dies at the hands of some other committee further on down the line'.[4]

Yet, effectively used, the committee is a valuable cog in the democratic machine. It provides the way through which the librarian and the elected council members can work together for the benefit of the library service and the community it serves. The committee meeting can provide the chief librarian (in some authorities senior members of staff as well) with a very real opportunity to influence the decisions that are finally taken.

Local circumstances vary. In some authorities officers can only speak in committee when invited to do so, in others they can contribute more or less freely to discussions. Let us now consider how the librarian can make the most of the opportunities made available to her or him.

Committee reports

The task starts well before the committee itself, with the preparation of an appropriate report. In these days of corporate management, committee reports are often the subject of scrutiny by a chief executive and a board of directors. The librarian may or may not be a member of this team. It is not part of our present purpose to discuss whether Chief Executives should spend so much of their costly time dotting 'i's and crossing 'ts' but suffice it to say that a well-prepared report can save the directors time and reduce councillors' capacity for misunderstandings.

A committee report is a unique and, within local government, a very important medium of communication. Before discussing the committee itself let us devote a few paragraphs to the art of preparing effective reports. During my time with the London Borough of Lambeth, one of my fellow assistant directors, Michael Perry, issued a useful set of notes on report preparation. Although these were intended for internal consumption, the ideas contained in them are generally applicable and I have used them as a basis for the following section.

The first thing to remember is that, by and large, the councillors who read a report will not have the same depth of knowledge of the subject as the writer of the report. It is essential, therefore, to make sure that full background information is provided in respect of all subject matter referred to in the report. At the same time, professional jargon should be removed, so as to enable the layman to understand the contents fully.

Structure

Some local authorities have a prescribed layout for committee reports and, where appropriate, this will have to be followed. Generally though, the main body of a report should indicate the reason for the paper, outline the main points of the argument, and lead to logical conclusions and (possibly) recommendations. Accuracy, brevity, and clarity are the all-important rules of report writing. The standard of local government reports is fairly low and it is to be hoped that librarians, who should be among the more literate of local government officers, can do something to raise the standard and so produce clear effective reports for their controlling committees.

The introduction to a report should give a brief history of the background of the matter under discussion and should refer members to any previous reports on the topic. Next should follow a logical and fair exposition of the facts and any argument or counter-argument. The reasons behind any suggestion should be made clear to the reader and vague generalizations avoided. Included *inter alia* should be a discussion of any legal implications (as for example in a report on library charges) and a mention of any financial considerations, such as the possibility of a government grant. In some cases, it may be more appropriate for a financial statement to take the form of an appendix. The costs of producing a local studies publication could, for instance, be presented in this way.

Keep the reader in mind

It is always wise to read through a report one has written, adopting the point of view of a councillor. This will help, not just to erase professional jargon, but also to highlight any questions that are raised by, but not answered in, the text. Statements such as 'surveys have shown' or 'it is essential that' raise obvious questions in the mind of a reader. If they are answered in the report it is less likely that they will be articulated in the committee meeting.

Some issues may have to be reported to more than just the committee responsible for library services. For example, matters with staffing implications would have to be reported to a Management Services Committee (or its local equivalent). Planning proposals, for instance a report on a new branch library, would have to go to a Planning and Development Committee. Reports with certain financial implications might have to go to a Finance Committee. On such matters, and indeed on many others, it will be necessary for the librarian responsible for the report to consult with fellow local government officers. It is good internal public relations and sound management for a report writer to make contact with staff in other departments, who have an interest in the subject under discussion.

Presentation

The visual presentation of information is as important in a committee report as it is in a strictly promotional publication. Local practice varies but in most cases a report should be given a heading. This should be unambiguous and indicate clearly the nature of the item under discussion. In order to attract the interest of specific councillors, it is useful to include after the heading the name of the ward or wards with which a report is particularly concerned. Such a reference would not, of course, be required in reports on subjects of general significance within the authority.

Some indication should also be given of the function of the report. This can be achieved by marking it 'For information', 'For decision', or whatever. Where recommendations are included they should be clearly set out in full at the end of the report. It is necessary to do this even if a recommendation is implicit in the body of the paper. It is, after all, just possible that some busy councillors may not have read all of the argument.

In addition to matters of local importance, it is necessary to keep committees informed of major developments in the library world. Any major report from the Department of Education and Science or similar body should be summarized and brought to members' attention. For those who want to read further, the full document should be placed in the Members' Library.

The same is generally true of Library Association policy statements. However, the local political climate may well determine the precise use that a chief librarian makes of such documents. In deciding what to present to committee, and how to present it, he or she has to exercise careful judgement as a 'political manager'.

In committee

Just what has to be taken to committees varies greatly from one authority to another and I do not propose to comment on that here. However, whatever is taken should be presented in the most effective and lucid way.

Visual aids

A written report can sometimes be supported by a visual presentation of information. The plans of a proposed new library are an obvious example, but less dramatic matters can also be promoted in this way. For example, during my period with the London Borough of Lambeth, we planned to produce reproductions of some local postcards as part of a series of local studies publications. We wanted to retain the sepia quality of the originals and had to persuade the committee of the worth of the extra costs involved in this process. In addition to my conventional report setting out the case, costs, and considerations, our very able graphic artist mounted a little display showing the original cards that we intended to use. As the members viewed these before the meeting, it became clear that there would be no opposition to the idea. In fact it was welcomed as an initiative.

The presentation of a scheme is common in commercial concerns but it is a technique that is not used to the full in local government. I came across a variation on this theme when in the United States. In the boardroom of the Cincinnati Library there was a display of press cuttings concerning the library. Board members were thus able to see what had been written about the library since their last meeting.

Speaking in committee

If a librarian is invited to speak during a committee meeting she or he should remember some of the basic rules of public speaking. So, if you are invited to contribute, take care to look at all the members while you are speaking, watch out for the non-verbal signals, search out and be sensitive to their reactions and be aware of the relationships between members. Above all, make what you are

In the boardroom of the Cincinnati Public Library – a display of press cuttings about the library. Board members can see the return, in single-column inches, of the library's public relations activities. (*Photo: Author*)

saying seem relevant to their interests and say it in terms that can be understood by the layman.

When making a case, you should look for possible areas of agreement and try to develop them. If you sense trouble on the horizon, you should adjust your arguments, perhaps repeating some of the key facts and restating the relevance of what you are saying in terms of the members and their interests.

Group behaviour

When speaking to a committee, the librarian can perhaps make use of her or his knowledge of group dynamics, transactional analysis, assertion training, or other more common management skills, even

150 *The Visible Library*

if for the rest of the time in committee she or he can only observe group processes in action. During this century there have been numerous studies of groups and group behaviour. A review of these is outside the scope of what is intended as a practical text. However, groups of one kind or another play such an important part in library life that a familiarity with some of these studies will not only aid the librarian in committee, but in all the other meetings that a librarian is called upon to attend. Most library school management courses now include reference to groups and, for those wishing to pursue the subject further, a few suggested sources are listed at the end of this chapter.[5]

Preparation

It should thus be clear that a chief librarian and any other member of staff attending a committee needs to prepare thoroughly for the event. There are one or two individuals who can charm a committee 'off the cuff'. They are rare, and for the rest of us lesser mortals the only way is to prepare our case and our presentation in advance of the meeting. This will enable 'the librarian [to] feel or appear easy and confident, on top of his job, but not on top of his committee'.[6] The last point is even more important today than when it was written. Many of the current breed of councillors do appear to be, from press reports at least, quite sensitive as to their status in relation to the professional officer.[7]

Open meetings

Under the 1972 Local Government Act, council and committee meetings have to be open to the press and general public, except where this would prejudice the public interest. Sub-committee meetings are not covered by this requirement and are only 'open' in some authorities. In addition, the law requires that public notice of council and committee meetings must be given at least three days in advance and that newspapers should, on request, be provided with advance copies of the agenda. The act also requires that reasonable reporting facilities be provided.

Some local government officers and some elected members are of the opinion that a press and public presence can inhibit discussion. However, there is still such a general misunderstanding of much of local government that any way in which the local decision-making process can be made more open is surely to be welcomed. For the librarian, the presence of the press does provide a further opportunity for putting the library case across — even if it is lost in the committee. This point has certainly not been lost on minority parties who often fight vigorously a case they know they are going to lose, in the hope of obtaining sympathetic press coverage.

The art of persuasion

The librarian is of course in a quite different position from the elected committee members who often argue a point from a party political viewpoint. The librarian can offer professional advice and information. Nevertheless, the able officer will present this in such a way that the strength of the argument will 'persuade' the committee to take the 'right' decision or, if they don't, convince the press and via them the public that the decision taken was the wrong one.

The librarian has to try and convince the powers that be of the importance of the library service. Although she or he must be able to work within the political structure of the committee, the skilful librarian leads and initiates. He or she should also cultivate those councillors who have a particular interest in the library service. As the former 'Bible' of English local government puts it: 'It is neither unknown nor improper for the official to have especially sympathetic relations with those members of the committee who show a predilection for his view of things'.[8] The limits of such a special relationship are a matter of judgement for the librarian concerned, but he or she should never show favouritism when dealing with individual elected members.

Perks

Many younger members of staff are unhappy at the perks given to council or committee members. In my youth I was no exception. Some of my earliest memories of perks include the existence of a privileged borrowers' file at the library where I started my career, and the local committee chairman who would descend on the branch looking for new thrillers. These could not be just any thrillers: they had to be British and not have a woman on the front!

At that time I not only disliked the chairman's criteria for book selection but also his apparent abuse of his position. However, over the years the political realities of local government life lead me to believe that it is a foolish librarian who does not look after the chairperson and members. At Lambeth, we always had a selection of books and records at the committee meeting for members to borrow and this was certainly appreciated.

To be fair, most elected representatives work hard and probably deserve the few perks they obtain. Also, before we adopt a 'holier than thou' attitude we should perhaps admit that most staff enjoy a few library perks as well. The service to the community will certainly not be harmed, and will probably benefit, if members are permitted to enjoy slightly special treatment. Some worldly-wise librarians would also include the chief executive and other senior officers in the 'slightly special service' category.

At a wider level, the librarian can increase the political awareness of library services through contact with the Association of County Councils (ACC) and the Association of Municipal Authorities (AMA). Communicating with local legislators is a vital public relations job. It falls mainly to the chief librarian and his or her senior staff to keep members of the controlling body informed, so that they can do the necessary persuading in council, and in other places where the library service may be competing for financial and other resources.

NOTES AND REFERENCES

1 Pennell, H B and others, *Find out who your friends are,* The Friends of the Free Library of Philadelphia Inc., 1978.

2 Corbett, E V 'Leisure a liability?' in Usherwood, R C (ed.) *Libraries and leisure,* AAL, South East Division, 1979.
3 Greenwood, R and others, *In pursuit of corporate rationality. Organisation developments in the post reorganisation-period,* INLOGOV, University of Birmingham,
4 Bales, R F 'In conference', *Harvard Business Review* 32(2), 1954.
5 Most introductory texts on social psychology contain information on group processes and group problem-solving. The following titles are but few from a large and growing literature:
Bion, W R *Experience in groups,* Tavistock, 1961.
Cartwright, D & Zander, A (eds) *Group dynamics: research and theory* 3rd ed., Tavistock, 1968.
Davis, J H *Group performance,* Addison–Wesley, 1969.
Shaw, M E *Group dynamics: the psychology of small group behaviour,* McGraw-Hill, 1971.
6 Savage, E A *The Librarian and his committee,* Grafton, 1942.
7 Recently one has heard of councillors discouraging librarians from providing community information that might circumvent local authority policy. From the new Wandsworth Council we have seen quite explicit statements by the elected members indicating that, where they feel it appropriate, they will overrule the professional judgement of their officers.
8 Finer, H *English local government* 4th ed. revised, Methuen, 1950.

Part Four

Considerations

'Today's fund seeking librarian would do well to be a cross between P T Barnum and Muhammad Ali. A more aggressive philosophy of librarianship is needed . . .'

Frederick Glazer, Selling the library, *1974*

Chapter 13
Managing Library Public Relations

Public relations is an integral part of the public library management process. Not only is public relations an essential management tool, it is also, in part, a result of management activity. Every management decision that is taken by a librarian will effect his or her library's relationship with its publics. Public relations, like any other area of management, needs to be carefully planned and costed. However, before discussing this matter, let us look at some of the other factors that need to be considered when managing a public library's public relations.

Staff attitudes

For public relations to be totally successful, the senior library staff have to be persuaded of its value. The senior management team has to believe that public relations can assist in achieving library objectives. It is only when top management appreciate the value of positive public relations that its full impact is felt. It is particularly important for the chief decision-makers in the library organization to realize that their decisions will affect the image of the library. Thus, in addition to the paid officers valuing PR, it is essential that there is the political will on the part of elected members to make use of public relations methods.

Local authority PR departments

In the past decade, urged on by Skeffington,[1] Maud,[2] and Baines,[3] local authorities in general have increased their public relations activities. Many now have specialized Public Relations Departments to advise both elected members and officers. Such departments normally include a press office which issues press releases and generally deals with press matters. In some authorities it is insisted that all press enquiries are handled by the press office and not by the individual departments.

This is part of the corporate dimension of modern local government public relations. Like much of corporate management this has advantages and disadvantages for the public librarian. On the one hand, it means that PR is handled by one or more public relations professionals. On the other, the fact that library publicity has to be channelled through an intermediary can put a further barrier between the library and the audience for which it is intended.

The relationships between the library department and the authority's PR Department are in themselves quite crucial. It is the librarian's responsibility to give the PRO advance warning of events, publications, and other matters that he or she wants publicized. Where, as in Lambeth, the Public Relations Department produces a newspaper of its own, this can provide the library service with an extra channel of communication.

A number of librarians, however, have expressed the view that the library's message can sometimes be swamped by the other duties of a local authority's Public Relations Department. Much of British local government PR is concerned with matters such as anti-litter campaigns, or promotions to stop dogs fouling footpaths, or producing posters to persuade people to pay their rates on time. These are of course important subjects, but one wonders if library publicity might not suffer through being associated with them in the mind of the public. In one local authority, such was the feeling against the library being swallowed up in the corporate identity, that the library staff designed, promoted, and used their own departmental logo in preference to that of the parent authority. There is the further point as to whether public relations staff, more used to designing campaigns of the 'stop dogs fouling footpath' variety, are the best-equipped people to promote the rather different library message.

Library PR departments

In the United States, as already indicated, many libraries have their own Public Relations Departments, some employing specialist journalists, artists, photographers and broadcasters. In a paper prepared for the 1978 ALA pre-conference on library public relations, Kathleen Rummel[4] suggested that a library with 50 to 100 full-time equivalent (FTE) staff should have 2 FTE persons assigned to PR, while in a library with 100 FTE staff and above there should be 'a base of 2 FTE persons assigned to PR with one additional staff person for every 100 staff'.

In the British public library context, separate Public Relations Departments simply do not exist. Some authorities, such as Leicestershire, have posts designated for a PR librarian, while others employ publications officers (e.g., Sheffield) and graphic designers (e.g., Shropshire County). With the exception of the graphic designers, most of these posts have been filled by professional librarians rather than by people professionally qualified in public relations.

There are some advantages in employing professional PR personnel. In general, the press and broadcasting organizations prefer dealing with fellow journalists. The media organizations also tend to feel that a professional public relations person will prepare and present material in the right form for them to use. It is also true that a PR professional is, initially at least, likely to have more contacts than a librarian entering the work for the first time.

Both professional librarians and professional public relations people should have communication skills, and there is no doubt that the right kind of librarian can do a very effective PR job. In addition, library public relations does require a person who can understand the library and its functions. Whoever undertakes library PR must be the type who can take the initiative. He or she must also possess sound judgement and really believe in the importance of the library client. Good public relations is not just a matter of informing people about the library and its services, it is also very much about listening to people, to their ideas, enquiries, and complaints.

Volunteers

Some public relations activities lend themselves to the employment of volunteer labour. For example, some libraries use trained volunteers as tour guides. Quite reasonably, trade union members object to volunteers doing a job that should be carried out by paid members of staff. For the sake of good staff/management relationships, consultations with appropriate union representatives should always take place before unpaid help is employed.

Training

It is the task of management to ensure that all staff are aware of the importance of public relations. There may be resistance on the part of some librarians who think that public relations is merely a series of circus acts below their professional dignity. The full function of positive public relations should be explained to them; in particular it is necessary to emphasize the importance of human relations.

The earlier this is done the better. Every induction programme for new staff should include a section on dealing with people. A course designed for a new assistant might include all or some of the following:

1. An explanation of the library's policy on everyday matters, such as smoking, wheelchairs, rowdyism, dogs, etc.
2. A session on how to deal with complaints and when to refer them to more senior members of staff.
3. The use of the telephone.
4. Local bylaws.
5. Interpretation of rules and regulations.

Above all, such a course should stress the importance of high standards of service and behaviour.

In addition to induction courses, some libraries include public relations in their general training programmes. Training can play a part in changing staff attitudes to PR. However, this is a long-term process and it would be foolish to suggest that entrenched attitudes can be changed by just one course. As convenor of the Sheffield Libraries Coordinating Committee's Working Party on Training and Education, the writer was involved in the presentation of a course on library public relations. The course itself was very successful, but a number of participants made the point that the people who would have most benefited from it did not attend. This is perhaps an example of selective exposure mechanisms at work within our own field! In recent years Buckinghamshire and Shropshire County Libraries have both devoted their annual training courses to public relations, making use of their own staff and outside speakers. In general, however, public relations has not featured in enough internal or external training courses.

For the librarian considering mounting a training programme in the field, there are a number of aids available. The Video Arts[4] films featuring John Cleese are both entertaining and instructive. In particular, I would recommend *Awkward customers* and *The meeting of minds*. Case studies and role-playing exercises can also be used with some effect. With a little thought, it is possible to write one's own case studies, but for those who do not wish to do so there are a number of published collections.[5] Role-playing exercises are a particularly good way of making staff aware of the difficulties and frustrations that can be experienced by the public in their attempts to use libraries.

Attitudes

The staff manual should also include a section on public relations. Indeed, the philosophy of PR should permeate all sections of the manual, especially those dealing with rules and regulations; management should decide just how many rules and regulations are really necessary. Restrictive regulations should be kept to a minimum and where rules do exist, staff should be encouraged to interpret them liberally. Very often junior staff can appear unnecessarily bureaucratic to the client, not because it is in their nature but because they do not have the confidence to bend the rules. It is up to senior management to encourage staff to give people priority over petty procedures. Too many public services in Britain seem to be organized to catch the 1 per cent who abuse them, rather than to help the 99 per cent who want to use them.

Libraries need not, and should not, be organized in this way. It is up to senior staff to set the right style.

One is both encouraged and discouraged by the views of chief librarians on this subject. The diversity of approach is well illustrated by the discussion that took place at a recent meeting of chief librarians. At one extreme there were those who were advocating a new and complicated procedure for registering out-of-authority readers, while on the other there were those who, quite rightly, wanted to make joining any library service as simple as possible. It is worth emphasizing that this was a meeting at which the librarians were free from direct political constraints and could express their own views. In so doing, they demonstrated their own attitudes towards the public they serve — attitudes which they are also, no doubt, communicating directly and indirectly to their staff.

No doubt, those who advocated stricter control of membership did so on the basis that they would be saving public money. This in itself is arguable, but what is more significant is the costs of such a policy, to individual library systems and to librarianship as a whole, in terms of public relations. For those members of the public faced with such a petty restriction, the library becomes just another bureaucratic organization placing barriers between the client and the service he or she requires. The person who is already suspicious or frightened of local authorities may not try to join again.

Costs

This is not to say that costs are not important: no one would argue that in today's economic climate. Library management needs to be aware of the costs of public relations, but equally it needs to be aware of the costs of not allocating resources to public relations — costs such as lack of public interest or decreased public and political support for the library service.

Public relations rarely appears as a separate budget item in a British public library's estimates. In fact, such a heading is relatively rare in the United States where, as I was told, there is a tendency to call it something else. Also in the US many libraries include programming (talks, film shows, concerts, etc.) under the same heading as public relations. This makes an assessment of the size of the 'pure' PR budget difficult. Rummel[6] suggests that 'a rule of thumb is that 10–15% of your budget should be applied to public relations, community relations, and programming'.

When calculating the costs of public relations, it is important to include all the costs involved. For example, the costs of issuing a press release will include some or all of the following:

1 The cost of posting x number of copies.
2 A percentage of the cost of the office equipment used to prepare and reproduce the releases.
3 The cost of stationery used.
4 The costs of any photographs included with the release.
5 Staff costs (time spent creating and writing the release, time spent typing the release, time spent duplicating, etc.).

With PR as with any aspect of management, it is vital to know how and why money has been spent.

Planning

Expenditure on public relations has to be carefully planned. Indeed, planning and preparation can make or break a library's public relations activities. PR should be planned to achieve clearly defined objectives. The planning process needs to include a consideration of the human and other resources available to help attain these objectives, an estimate of the financial resources required, and an indication of target dates for achieving objectives. Priorities will, of course, have to be established within any given timetable.

Once overall objectives and priorities have been ascertained and consideration given to the resources needed, the library public relations person is in a position to consider specific matters of detail. As part of this process it is necessary to look at the library service through the eyes of the library's various publics. Clients, staff, non-users, legislators, and suppliers will all have different perceptions of the library and its services. For each of

164 *The Visible Library*

these groups the library will have, in balance-sheet terms, PR assets and PR liabilities. Senior library management should seek to identify these assets and liabilities as an integral part of their public relations planning.

In a typical public library, assets might include helpful assistants, an accessible location, a reliable reference service, and so on. Liabilities could include belligerent staff, erratic overdue procedures, negative notices, and the like. One of the functions of library PR is to reduce such liabilities to a minimum. By paying close attention to all aspects of the service, it is possible to draw up a public relations balance sheet listing those things which help and those which hinder the library's image.

On the basis of such preparation, one can begin to produce a practical programme of activities tailored to the library's needs and resources. It will be necessary to plan some things well in advance, but a PR programme also needs to be flexible, so that the library service can quickly respond to new events and demands.

As a vital part of a library's internal public relations it is essential to involve staff in the public relations planning process. As stated earlier, there may be staff who are suspicious of the value of the whole idea and it is especially necessary to secure their cooperation and support. There is no easy way of doing this but certainly it will be much more difficult if plans are announced to them without any warning.

NOTES AND REFERENCES

1 Department of the Environment *People and planning,* The Skeffington Report, HMSO, 1969.
2 *Report of the committee on the management of local government,* The Maud Report, HMSO, 1967.
3 Study Group on Local Authority Management Structures *The new local authorities: Management and structure,* The Baines Report, HMSO, 1972.
4 A catalogue detailing Video Arts training films is available from Video Arts Ltd, Dumbarton House, 68 Oxford St, London W1N 9LA. The company also organizes regular presentations of films throughout the U.K.

5 See for example:
  Kies, C *Problems in library public relations*, Bowker, 1974.
6 Rummel, K K 'PR Planning/budgeting/evaluation' in Moran, I (comp.) *The library public relations recipe book*, Public Relations Section, Library Administration Division, American Library Association, 1978.

Chapter 14
Evaluating Library Public Relations

'*Some kinds of* communication *on some kinds of* issues *brought to the attention of some kinds of* people *under some kinds of* conditions *have some kinds of* effects.' Bernard Berelson.[1]

Berelson wrote those words in 1948. Today, after three more decades of mass communications research, we still have to admit that it is very difficult to evaluate accurately the results of a public relations campaign or programme. Some people feel that it is not practical to measure the results of library promotional activities. It is certainly very difficult to isolate the effects of library public relations from those of other library management activities.

It is difficult but not impossible. The real problem is that the cost of such measurement may be greater than the cost of the public relations effort itself. To measure the results of a campaign, which attempted to change public attitudes and opinions towards the library service, would require quite sophisticated and expensive research. It would be even more difficult and costly to try and measure the long-term cumulative effects of public relations.

In some respects, public relations is an act of faith. One of the functions of PR is to act as an insurance against the future. Thus, a library service wants to keep its publics informed, not just for immediate short-term benefits, but also for a future time when it may need their help and support. During my tour of the United States I asked every public relations librarian, 'How do you evaluate your results?' The most common reply to my question can be summed up in the response, 'We hope it does some good'.

Faith and hope, then, play a large part in the PR person's philosophy. There is, however, little room for charity. Library public relations does have to justify itself. Certainly, a library committee, spending ratepayers' money on library publicity and promotion, will want some indication of the possible benefits of PR to the library and the community it serves.

Of course, before any kind of evaluation can be attempted, it is necessary to know what any particular public relations activity was intended to achieve. As we saw from the previous chapter, part of PR planning is to set objectives and targets. No public relations activity should be embarked upon without a clear understanding of what the library hopes to gain from it.

The means by which such objectives might be achieved have been discussed in the earlier part of the book. The precise nature of the 'measure' of their effectiveness will obviously vary with the kind of activity undertaken. In the following paragraphs some possible methods of evaluation are discussed. Some of these have been used by American library organizations and others have been tried by commercial public relations concerns on both sides of the Atlantic. In my view, none of the methods described is rigorous enough to give anything more than a general indication of the success or failure of any particular public relations activity.

Such a lack of precision is not just a problem in library public relations but in public relations in general. As two leading PR consultants write: 'The public relations profession is striving for practical, universally applicable methods of evaluation, but it must be freely admitted that for the time being the practitioner and the management are obliged to put their faith in personal observation and empirical evidence of the many public relations programs which have been followed by good results'.[2]

Media exposure analysis

A number of American libraries have used various forms of media exposure analysis to measure the success or failure of their press and broadcasting relations. Press cuttings are one yardstick by which a librarian can evaluate his or her public relations activities. If press releases consistently fail to be published, it may be that there is something wrong with the nature of the release or that they are being sent to inappropriate newspapers and magazines.

A very simple measure is simply to count the single-column centimetres of coverage received by the library in the press. Though this will tell you little more than that the library received so many centimetres of coverage, such an analysis can usefully be taken further by examining the type of publication in which the library service does, or does not, obtain coverage.

When evaluating radio and television coverage, some libraries in the United States keep a detailed record of all those stations that carry library material, noting the amount of air time devoted to the library service. The report of one library's Public Relations Department contains an itemized listing of radio and television placements and details of the number of stations carrying 'spot announcements'. Another library gathers information from local radio and television stations on their usage of library publicity material. A suitably disguised example of this kind of subjective assessment is reproduced on page 169.

Records can also be kept of the number of people who attend a library promotional event, such as the showing of a library film, though there is some evidence to suggest that the people who attend such events tend already to be well informed about the service or topic being promoted.[3] In general, it is very important to remember that media exposure analysis only shows the extent to which a public relations item has been used by the media. The fact that a library's message has been disseminated does not by any means guarantee that it has had any effect.

The success or otherwise of a public relations activity does not just depend on the campaign itself, but also on the audience for it. Even when a library has been successful in 'reaching' the public with a message, people still have to interpret that message for themselves. Individual psychological, sociological, and geographical factors will cause some people to discount, distrust, or simply ignore the message. An individual's selective exposure mechanisms can determine just what information he or she pays attention to. It is not unknown for people to avoid actively some forms of information (if you are a smoker how do you react to anti-smoking campaigns?), while others may be simply apathetic. A number of public information campaigns designed to promote some most worthy causes have floundered because of such audience factors.

Radio-TV Station	1976 Total Usage	Comments
WCLA-TV	25 PSAs	
WLA	unable to determine	Material is used regularly, but person in charge during 1976 is in hospital.
WLA	$13,239. air time reported for May through October	Joan Lister will gather information from daily log and call with figures.
WKLA-TV	none	This station uses no PSAs.
WKLA	48 PSAs	*Community Datebook* uses information the day before the event.
WXLA-TV	unable to determine	PSAs used at sign on and sign off each day. 'Don't keep records, but we use most of it,' said Cindy Lewis.
WKYL-FM	312 PSAs	'Six times a week, on the average.'
WEBU	312 PSAs	'We use everything you send us,' on *Community Datebook* which airs 3 times each day. Estimates 6 times each week.
WNRU	312 PSAs	'Average 6 PSAs a week for you; more and longer announcements for Jazz Live.'
WLRU	624 PSAs	'Average 2 a day for 6 days a week on *Community Calendar*. Some weeks we use more, some weeks there are space limitations.' Tania Stevens.
WFPF-FM	365 PSAs	'We use them all the time, especially films, on the average of one a day.'
WAPG-FM	730 PSAs	'... read all the PSAs we get daily from 6:30 to 7 p.m. Copy is at announcers hand during our entire broadcast day.'
WLRU-FM	365 PSAs	'At least one a day, we're on the air all year long now.' Brian Old.
WCEG	156 PSAs	'Terrific,' says Julie Lang 'we use 3 a week with a colour slide.'

Surveys

In exceptional cases, a library service may wish to commission a survey of clients' attitudes before and after a campaign or promotion. Opinion research is, however, likely to be expensive but it is a false economy to attempt to do such work 'on the cheap'. The results obtained from a badly designed questionnaire or poor interviewing are likely to be worse than useless in that they may well be misleading. Personal feedback from clients, councillors, and community leaders may provide information which may be more useful in assessing the library's public standing.

The increase in the use of a library's services following a publicity campaign may be a measure of the effect of a campaign, but not necessarily so. It will require quite sophisticated research techniques to isolate the effects of a campaign from all the other internal and external factors that may, or may not, have led to an increase in the use of a service. When attempting to measure the effects of public relations, one must beware of confusing correlation with causation.

Coupons and write-ins

With some public relations activities it is possible to encourage audience response directly. For example, a coupon can be included with a publication inviting readers to mail a comment or request to the library. New York Public Library has used this technique to measure the effectiveness of its direct mail publications. This particular method can lead to very biased responses and any results need to be interpreted with great caution. Similar techniques can be used to measure the audience for a library radio programme. The most common method is to include a write-in competition as part of the show.

Economic indications

Public relations persons working in those American libraries that directly campaign for budget support believe, not surprisingly,

Fund-raising on the steps of the New York Public Library. The size of the dollar contribution is an indicator to the effectiveness of such a campaign. (*Photo: Author*).

that the percentage vote by which the budget is approved or rejected gives some indication of the success or failure of their efforts. This is still only a partial indicator, because the budget vote can be affected by other matters. This was certainly the case in 1978 when some libraries' budgets were rejected, not because of a poor campaign, but rather as the result of a well-orchestrated populist movement against the property tax.

In Britain, individual librarians and library organizations are currently mounting a campaign against cuts in public expenditure. The result of their efforts might be public action or apathy, but whatever it is it will be very difficult to separate out each of the factors leading to the public's response. This is not — repeat not — to say that we believe such a campaign will have no effect, but simply to emphasize that we do not yet have resources to evaluate and demonstrate the precise nature of that effect.

172   *The Visible Library*

Fund-raising campaigns may be more directly evaluated by reference to the size of the dollar contributions, though, no doubt, an individual or group donation may also depend on external economic factors.

Research

Few of the methods indicated above can provide librarians with a conclusive evaluation of a public relations programme. There is, therefore, a need for much more research into the effects of library promotional activities, because the image of a library service is far too important a matter to be left to chance.

Research is needed at both the micro and the macro level. There is a need to answer operational questions about such things as the success or otherwise of a library exhibit, or the extent of press coverage, but also we need to study public attitudes to libraries and to examine the nature of the criticism of library services. We have no way of really knowing if criticisms of library services derive from the services themselves, populist views about public expenditure, or simply — or rather complicatedly — lack of knowledge. It may be that attitudes to a service change with time. Trend studies of attitudes to libraries might help us find out.

Research in this area is not going to provide quick or easy answers but that should not prevent its being carried out. Most of the research that has been done on the effectiveness of library public relations activities has been at the micro, rather than the macro level. For example, in 1967 Rediffusion television looked at the effect of a television programme, *Best sellers*. Using libraries in Westminster and Lewisham, a comparison was made of the number of titles borrowed from libraries making special efforts to promote the authors mentioned in the programme, and the number of titles borrowed from a 'control' library where no special efforts were made.

The British Library Research and Development Department has funded some studies of PR techniques. One based in Newcastle attempted to evaluate the effects of promotional techniques on library use, in particular that of small service points.[4] Another, as mentioned in chapter 9, investigated direct mail advertising as a method of 'selling' the library.[5] Although both were interesting and well-documented experiments, their results were somewhat inconclusive.

In Sweden, as Greta Renborg[6] has reported, a few attempts have been made to evaluate public relations activities, particularly those aimed at the non-user. In the United States, Sue Fontaine's study[7] was intended 'to examine the state of the art of public relations in selected public libraries'. Her report does look at evaluation but reflects the lack of rigorous measurement techniques that we have noted elsewhere. The commentary to the tape-slide presentation developed from the study states: 'How do you measure public relations successes or failures? . . . It's public opinion that counts. Increased use of the library . . . and increased support in terms of dollars tell how well we are doing our job'.[8]

Also from the United States comes a report of a pilot project to 'illustrate the effectiveness of a tailor-made public relations campaign'. This was centred on Adel Public Library, serving a population of 2,500, and was primarily concerned with the effectiveness of library community relations. The public relations officer for the State Library Commission of Iowa has no doubts about the success of Adel's community relations programme. She reports: 'Hundreds of new users . . . circulation has increased dramatically . . . more funding from the city . . . organizations are contributing money for a new film projector and screen . . . a slide projector has been donated . . . volunteers renovated the basement . . . and a Friends group has been formally organized'.[9] These are very positive results and it is to be hoped that the effect of the campaign is continuing and that such good results can be duplicated elsewhere.

Few librarians have felt able to be so sure about the effects of their public relations efforts because, as we have noted elsewhere, the evaluation of PR is a difficult and expensive task. However, it is also a necessary one. It is essential to evaluate library public relations in order to establish just how far a library has reached in achieving its promotional objectives. In addition, such evaluation should be an integral part of the planning process for future public relations activities.

174 *The Visible Library*

The evaluation of library services has long been a concern of the Public Libraries Research Group. As part of its current work on public library performance measures, the group has produced a statement on library public relations. This statement, which is reproduced below, is based on an outline submitted to the group by the author.

Public Libraries Research Group
Public Relations Value Statement

Objectives

1 To establish and maintain mutual understanding between the ... public library and its publics.
2 To influence favourably public and government attitudes and opinions regarding the ... public library.
3 To increase the general awareness of services provided by the ... public library.
4 To build public confidence in the service provided by the ... public library.

Need

This will vary from community to community but under this heading one might include topics such as:

> Percentage use of the library service
> Favourable/unfavourable media coverage
> Percentage allocation of local authority budget, etc.

Methods by which objectives might be achieved

1 By means of a deliberately planned and sustained public relations programme.
2 By appointing ... staff to plan, organize, and develop the public relations programme.
3 By identifying the target audience for each promotional activity.
4 By means of printed and other publications.
5 Through liaison with the local press, radio, and television.
6 By means of display inside and outside library premises.
7 Through liaison with community leaders and groups within the community.
8 By means of participation in exhibitions, country fairs, county shows, etc.

9 Through liaison with professional associations.
10 By use of paid advertisements.
11 By training staff in interpersonal and other relevant skills

Evaluation of Library PR

NB The precise nature of any "measure" will vary with the type of activity.

1 Measures of the effects of a specific promotional activity.
   e.g. (i)   Increased use of service following the publication of a guide
   e.g. (ii) Books borrowed as the result of a display
   e.g. (iii) Increase in use by ethnic minorities following publication of brochure in minority languages.
2 Media exposure analysis.
   e.g. (i) Single column centimetres (S.C.C.) of coverage in local press
   e.g. (ii) Broadcast time on local radio
3 Attitude survey of clients, non users, members etc. before and after a campaign or promotion.
4 Questionnaires on the effectiveness of a P.R. activity.
5 A measurement of coupon response where appropriate (e.g. a coupon included with a publication). Beware of bias in responses.
6 Interviews to ascertain the degree of exposure or reaction to a particular campaign.
7 Pre-testing publications and/or campaigns.
                                                              etc.

Note

The important factor to note about PR is that it is *planned* and *continuous*. Having achieved the objectives set out at the beginning, and thus persuaded the public that library services are relevant to their needs, good public relations helps keep clients and supporters by persuading them that they have made the right decision.

McGarry and Burrell have identified six persuasive messages that can be used by librarians:[10]
1 *Social* appeal: *Everybody* uses the library!
2 *Prestige* appeal: *All the best people* use the library!
3 *Survival* appeal: *No-one can compete* in modern life without help from the library.

4 *Fun* appeal: Use the library for *fun and leisure*!
5 *Egomaniac* appeal: Knowledge is *power*!
6 *Fear* appeal: If you don't use the library your friends will *ostracize* you!

There are others, not the least of which is self-improvement, but it will need some careful research to identify which particular message will be most successful with a particular audience at a particular time.

NOTES AND REFERENCES

1 Berelson, B 'Communications and public opinion' in Schramm, W *Communications in modern society,* University of Illinois Press, 1948.
2 Yutzy, T D & Williams, S 'New perspective on public relations' in Lerbinger, O & A Sullivan, A J (eds) *Information, influence and communication,* Basic Books, 1965.
3 This was known at least thirty years ago. See for example: Cartwright, D 'Some principles of mass persuasion: selected findings on the sale of U.S. War Bonds' *Human Relations* 2, 1949, 253–67.
4 Woodhouse, R G *and* Neill, J *Promotion of public library use,* Department of Librarianship, Newcastle upon Tyne Polytechnic, (Occasional Paper No. 2), 1979 (BLR & D Report No. 5470).
5 Cronin, B *Direct mail advertising and public library use* (BLR & D Report No. 5539), British Library, 1980.
6 See:
Renborg, G 'Public relations activities for the Stockholm City Library' *Scandinavian Public Library Quarterly* 3, 1970.
Renborg, G *Bibliotekens P.R. — och kontaktarbete,* Berlings, Lund, 1977.
7 Fontaine, S *Report to the Council on Library Resources. Public relations in public libraries,* 1975.
8 Fontaine, S *Public relations tick/click.* A 30-minute slide presentation funded by the Council on Library Resources, 1975.
9 Stiles, F 'Community relations' in Moran, I (comp.) *The library public relations recipe book,* Public Relations Section, Library Administration Division, American Library Association, 1978.
10 McGarry, K J & Burrell, T W *Communication studies — a programmed guide,* Bingley, 1973.

Chapter 15
Public Relations for the Library Profession

The public relations activities of the individual public library have to be set against the general public view of the library profession. Improving the image and increasing the influence of librarianship is a role for professional associations. I am particularly concerned with this role so far as it affects public libraries. Somewhat late in its history, the Library Association is beginning to recognize the importance of public relations. It has recently set up a sub-committee, the aim of which is: 'To initiate and keep under review all aspects of the Association's public relations, with particular emphasis on the parliamentary lobby'.

Political PR

The emphasis on a parliamentary lobby is something to be welcomed. Political public relations is perhaps the most crucial job for a professional association to undertake. To do it justice, the Library Association has been quietly influential in this area for some time. Although the Public Lending Right debate was finally lost, it was kept going for far longer than most neutral observers would have expected. The LA also publicly opposed the idea of direct charges on users of public libraries, when it was floated by some senior members of the Tory party at the time of the 1970 General Election. The same idea was again mooted in 1979 but, at the time of going to press, (Autumn 1980) it appears that the Association has been successful in persuading the government against introducing legislation that would enable local authorities to charge user fees for library borrowings.

In the recent past, the LA also sponsored parliamentary amendments to attempt to exempt libraries from prosecution

Campaigning against the cuts. (*Library Association General Services poster*)

under a proposed Cinematograph and Indecent Display Bill. One of the concerns of the now disbanded public relations working party was to find a number of MPs willing to represent the Association's interests and to keep a weather eye on proposed legislation. The LA accordingly established a Parliamentary Sub-Committee and made arrangements to consult two MPs and a MEP; in addition, the LA has employed the services of a parliamentary agent, has access to a parliamentary information service and has joined the Parliamentary and Scientific Committee, which liaises between MPs and professional institutions.

The Association maintains close relationships with the Department of Education and Science. There are regular lunches at the LA which are attended by the library advisers and some senior civil servants. Library Association representatives also meet with the Minister for the Arts about three times a year and there are close contacts with the Association of Municipal Authorities and the Association of County Councils. In fact, the professional advisers to these local authority organizations tend to coordinate their activities via the Library Association. In addition, the Association liaises with the various trade unions concerned with library staff.

By submitting evidence to government and other committees concerned with library and library-related matters, the Association can significantly influence library legislation. In recent years, evidence has been supplied to committees considering a very wide range of topics. For instance, to the Williams Committee (on the laws dealing with obscenity), the Whitford Committee (on Copyright), and the Yates Committee (on recreation management training). It is difficult to evaluate the immediate impact of this kind of work, but there can be little doubt that over the years Library Association initiatives have led to better public library provision.

At the level of local politics, LA policy statements can, as has been indicated elsewhere, be usefully put before local committees. The secretariat could also provide a useful service by providing analysis of library issues for use by members in their own localities. In addition, there is no reason why the Association should not actively encourage members to write to local and

**cut
libraries
and see
wot
hapens**

LIBRARIES OPEN AND FREE   4 WOODLAND WAY   WELWYN   AL6 ORZ

Campaigning against the cuts. (*Libraries Open and Free (LOAF) poster*) national legislators. This could be done by letters — or rather formulas for letters — being produced by the Library Association for adaptation to individual use. (An American example of such a letter is reproduced in Chapter 12.)

It is our belief that members themselves have a professional responsibility to write to MPs and other influential people on library matters. Letter-writing and lobbying are a legitimate part of the decision-making process. Unlike their American colleagues, British librarians have been reluctant to involve themselves in such activities — perhaps because such political activity is regarded as unprofessional. However, if members of the public library profession are not willing to defend its standards and services, they cannot expect others to do so for them. As professionals, we should let legislators know our professional views loudly and clearly. The LA 'cuts' poster and the activities of the LOAF (Libraries Open and Free) organization are welcome signs that this is now beginning to happen.

The Library Association and its members

The Library Association's relations with its own membership has at times left something to be desired. In the past, there seems to have been rather less than 'mutual understanding' between the council and the membership at large. The McCrae proposition[1] for a £3 basic subscription, if nothing else, revealed a failure by the Association to explain itself to the membership. In order to help bridge the gap between Ridgmount Street and the country at large, members of the LA council and members of the secretariat undertake 'communication visits' to branches, groups, and sections, and also to library schools. In addition, LA council meetings have been open to members for some time, although unfortunately few make use of the opportunity to attend.

It is important that individual public librarians participate in the work of their professional association. Time spent working for the Library Association, the Association of Assistant Librarians, the Youth Libraries Group, and so on is time well spent. In their role as managers, senior librarians should actively encourage their staff to take part in the work of professional associations.

182 *The Visible Library*

Staff so involved will make valuable contacts in the library and communications worlds and, in my experience, they are also more likely to be aware of current developments in librarianship.

Promotion and publicity by the LA

Compared with its counterparts in the United States or Scandinavia, the British Library Association does relatively little to promote or publicize public libraries directly. The American Library Association adopts a multimedia approach to library promotion. It produces banners, posters, bookmarks, and public service announcements for radio and television. These are made available to library authorities at cost. Both the posters and the broadcast materials are designed so as to enable local libraries to add their own individual identification. The ALA also provides local libraries with a suggestion kit of publicity ideas, camera-ready copy of printed advertisements for local media or in-house use, and sample news releases. The money from the sale of these materials is reinvested in a national library public service campaign.

The ALA also places the radio and television materials with the national networks. Featuring well-known authors and show-business celebrities, such as Doris Day, Bob Newhart, and Dennis Weaver these, like all the other ALA materials, are professionally produced. Although it has not been possible to include recorded extracts from the radio spots within the format of this book, readers might like to know that they can sometimes be heard in Europe on the American Forces Network.

The Danish Library Association is also very active in the field of public relations. In 1960 it set up a full-time Public Relations Department which was partly funded by local authorities. These funds were only awarded for three years but 'it proved possible within this period to infuse the idea of libraries into the public mind to an extent unknown before'.[2]

At the end of the three-year period, the DLA set up a Public Relations Committee. This has produced promotional material, including films, and has mounted advertising campaigns. The

Dragon Poster 22"x31"

Cat Poster 22"x31"

"Wright Brothers" poster 18"x23¼"

"Billie Jean King" poster 18"x23¼"

Posters produced by the American Library Association.

Association also has a Radio and Television Committee and a special section which issues frequent notices to the press.

Our own Library Association is not a major producer of promotional material. True, it has produced booklists and bibliographies and once marketed a library display kit, but it could and should do so much more. The old public relations working party decided against the central production of library display and publicity material though my understanding is that the matter might be considered again. At the moment, the Association appears to be limiting itself to the distribution of the Public Libraries Group tie and tee shirts. The tie in itself is not a bad idea but given the number of women in the profession one wonders why a scarf was not also produced.

Other activities currently under consideration are, I understand, the award of a LA scholarship or bursary and ways of nominating members of the profession for the Queen's Birthday Honours List. These are worthy but rather unexciting committee ideas. Our professional association should do more.

In particular, it should be concerned with the quality of people recruited to the profession. It is reasonable to assume a relationship between the type of person attracted to a profession and that profession's public image. Although librarianship and information work continue to attract some of the best people from our schools and universities we cannot afford to remain complacent. Over the next few years we are likely to see the development of many new kinds of 'communications careers', with obvious implications for the library profession. At a general level, the Association needs to promote an image of librarianship and information work more in tune with the needs of our post-industrial society. Specifically, it should improve the format and content of the careers information emanating from its headquarters.

The LA also needs to be more adventurous in responding to the issues of the day. If it is to be a power in the land members of the LA secretariat and council must be more willing to comment on matters of controversy. One would hope that the media would look to the LA for comment on issues such as intellectual freedom or freedom of information. However, this is only going to happen if the Association is not afraid to 'make waves' occasionally.

However, some progress is being made: as already mentioned, the public relations working party has been replaced by the Public Relations Sub-Committee, and the Information Department has extended its area to include press liaison, its title, Information and Press Department, reflecting this change. The Information and Press Officer also represents the LA on the Freedom of Information Liaison Committee which meets regularly at the House of Commons.

The case for a LA public relations office

What the Library Association lacks is a full-time public relations office. In recent years the Association has spent significant sums of money on the services of various public relations consultants. The results, to say the least, have not been good. The attempts at a National Library Week and the later National Bookweek have only met with limited success, while the LA's centenary year passed virtually unnoticed by the nation at large. On that occasion, the PR consultants certainly failed to deliver the goods — though it has to be said that the PR objectives of that particular celebration were never adequately defined. It was never clear whether the event was to be used to promote the Library Association or libraries in general.

The appointment of a full-time public relations officer would help establish the LA in the eyes of the media as a familiar and trustworthy source of information about library matters. An LA public relations person could make those all-important contacts with the media; a full-time office could issue press releases and, at appropriate times, feed the media with statements and reactions from the president, secretary, and members of the council.

Although there are at present officers who concern themselves with all aspects of LA conferences and exhibitions, the creation of a full-time office would ensure that the most is made of the public relations opportunities provided by conferences and exhibitions. Before such events, pre-prints and summaries of papers, highlighting important or controversial points, should be provided to the press and broadcasting media. The presence of a national or local celebrity at a conference could be used to obtain maximum media coverage. It should also be within the power of the LA to provide local newspapers and radio stations with a list of people who can be approached to comment on library and library-related matters.

None of these comments is intended as a criticism of the present officers of the Association. They are, however, intended as a criticism of the resources made available to them. Effective public relations costs money — but wisely used it is money well invested. This is certainly the view of the Law Society which has recently seen fit to invest £400,000 in a national publicity campaign. The association for a profession which is concerned with the communication of information and ideas should surely feel it worth while to communicate information about itself, its members and their activities effectively.

It is my view that the Library Association should establish a public relations office. At the very least, public relations should be the responsibility of a full-time officer of the Association. A professional public relations person would be well suited to such a post, but a librarian with PR skills and sympathies might also usefully perform the job.

My views as to what the aims and activities of a Library Association Public Relations Department should be are summarized below:

Library Association Public Relations Department

Objectives

1. To inform interested and influential publics about the Library Association and the practice and philosophy of librarianship.
2. To establish and maintain mutual understanding between the Library Association and its publics.
3. To influence favourably public and government attitudes and opinions regarding the library profession.
4. To build and maintain public confidence in the services provided by librarians and by library organizations.

Description of (possible) services

1. *Media relations* To include liaison with press and broadcasting organizations, the production and distribution of news releases, the arrangement of press conferences and press facilities at conferences and meetings of council.
2. *Political relations* To promote a parliamentary lobby for library and library-related matters. To keep national and local legislators informed on library and library-related matters. To liaise with ministers and opposition spokespersons. To liaise with officers of the Department of Education and Science, and other government departments concerned with library and library-related matters. To promote and coordinate legislative campaigns.
3. *Book trade relations* To liaise with the book trade and in particular with organizations, such as the National Book League, the Booksellers Association, and the Publishers Association.
4. *Relations with communications organizations* To liaise with individuals and organizations concerned with the communication of information and ideas.
5. *Relations with educational organizations* To liaise with individuals and organizations concerned with all levels of full-time and part-time education.
6. *Relations with leisure and recreation organizations* To liaise with individuals and organizations concerned with leisure and recreation provision in both the public and private sectors.
7. *Trade Union relations* To liaise with those trade unions concerned with staff working in library and library-related organizations.
8. *Membership relations* To keep the membership fully informed regarding the activities of the LA council and committees. To create an awareness among the membership of the beneficial work of the Association and to explain the importance of this work.
9. *PR advice service* To provide professional public relations advice to members of council and committees, to the

membership at large, and to officers of the Association.
10 *Publicity and promotional material* To produce and distribute promotional material, e.g. posters, radio and television announcements, visual aids, booklists, display kits, etc. To provide members with professional advice on graphic design and the production of promotional material.
11 *Public opinion* To monitor public opinion regarding library and library-related matters.
12 *Evaluation* To evaluate the Association's public relations activities.
13 *PR archives* To maintain a record of the Association's public relations activities.

It is true that a number of these activities are already undertaken, to some extent, by various departments within the Association. However, it is my view that to make them the responsibility of a single department would bring them into sharper focus and provide a more obvious point of contact for external organizations. There would necessarily be a close relationship between the proposed Public Relations Department and those responsible for the LA's international relations.

Though not necessarily within the remit of the suggested Public Relations Department, I should also like to see the LA become more active in promoting research and training in library PR. One would hope for a time when a group of the Library Association is as active as the Public Relations Section of the Library Administration Division of the ALA, whose many activities help to promote an in-depth understanding of public relations within the library profession.

Outside the LA

There are other organizations, apart from professional library associations, whose public relations activities and interests can be of benefit to public libraries. These include the Booksellers Association, the National Book League, the Publishers Association, the Publishers Publicity Circle, and the Society of Young Publishers. Although it is necessary for each of these organizations to maintain their separate identities, there are times when a corporate public relations effort could be mutually beneficial.

In Britain, National Library Weeks and National Bookweeks have attempted PR work on behalf of the book and library world. At a national level, these were only partially successful. Their major successes were at a local level.

An example of a local event that had a national impact was the Bedford Square Bookbang which took place in London in June 1971. This took the form of a fair with tents, pavilions and even a big top and, despite taking place in a period of appalling weather, attracted some 43,000 visitors who bought some £12,000 (1971 prices) of books. However, not all visitors were entirely satisfied with the event and there was some criticism of the library profession's contribution: '. . . one little notice board with a few details about BNB! Couldn't we, as a profession, think of anything more enticing than that? As 'the image' of the librarian is one of the main topics of grievance . . . I feel that something a little better could have been arranged'.[3]

The image of the librarian is indeed a topic of grievance at professional gatherings. The American Library Association has been known to complain about the use of library stereotypes in advertisements. I am also reliably informed that the ALA has at times dissuaded companies from using advertisements presenting the stereotyped image. When the Nabisco company used such an ad., some American librarians formed LADLE (The Librarians' Anti-Defamation League). This *ad hoc* group marched on the company's headquarters complaining that the offending advertisement 'perpetuated the worn-out all-too-familiar stereotype — the librarian as a turn-of-the-century old bat'.[4] But perhaps we complain too loudly for, in the words of Jock Murison, it 'behoves us to remember that we did not get our awful public image by chance'.[5]

A more positive image is promoted by the Toy Libraries Association which sells itself through a variation on the Superman theme — Toyman. In addition, the TLA has also produced a useful pamphlet on 'how to start a community toy library' and packs of Christmas cards.

The positive image of the Toy Libraries Association.

John Cotton Dana Library PR Awards

The H W Wilson Company and the public relations section of the ALA's Library Administration Division have sponsored a library public relations award contest for over thirty years. This contest is named after John Cotton Dana who, in forty years as a practising librarian, did much to expand the services of libraries and, as the eleventh President of the American Library Association, undertook pioneering work to stimulate the use of library services.

The John Cotton Dana Award is open to libraries throughout the world and in recent years awards have been won by the London Borough of Camden and the London Borough of Islington. Printed materials and/or non-printed materials may be submitted. When considering entries the judges take into account the financial and other resources available to a library for PR activities. The fact sheet which has to accompany any entry is reproduced below and gives an indication of the judges' concerns. In order to give small library systems a chance, entries are judged on the quality of the information provided, rather than on expensive or flashy presentation.

At the time of going to press the British Library Association is seeking a sponsor for a library PR contest to be modelled on the John Cotton Dana Award.

International relations

PR for the library profession should not be restricted by national boundaries. There are some who would like to see the Library Association set up a separate International Relations Office and, given the potential range of the Association's international activities, this idea has much to commend it. The Association of Assistant Librarians has always been very active in this field, and over the years has played a significant part in building professional international relations at the individual level.

International professional associations, such as the Commonwealth Library Associatioin (COMLA), the Fédération Internationale de Documentation (FID), and the International Federation of Library Associations (IFLA,) are helping to promote the

JOHN COTTON DANA LIBRARY PUBLIC RELATIONS AWARDS CONTEST

FACT SHEET

SUBMIT THIS FACT SHEET WITH YOUR ENTRY when it is sent to The H. W. Wilson Company. If audiovisual material is part or all of your entry, the Audiovisual Fact Sheet must also be attached.

SENT FROM_____DATE_____
           (Organization)

ANSWERS TO ALL QUESTIONS MUST BE TYPED

1. Summarize the public relations program described in your entry including any unique aspects. (Approx. 25-50 words.) Use reverse of this sheet, if necessary.

2. State results which can be directly attributed to this public relations program.

3. For what audience was this public relations program intended?

4. Total operating budget._____
4a. Total public relations budget._____
5. Number of people you are expected to serve._____
   (Latest census figure, if public library)
6. Do you receive any outside support funds for your public relations program such as from The Friends of the Library, Service Clubs, etc.?

7. Total number of staff employed. Full time_____Part time_____
8. How many hours of volunteer help for the library?_____
9. Do you have a specific person assigned to handle your library's public relations program? YES_____NO_____
9a. How many staff members are assigned to public relations activities?
    Full time_____Part time_____Volunteer_____
10. How did you find out about this contest?_____
    _____

PLEASE ANSWER ALL QUESTIONS

The John Cotton Dana 'fact sheet' (*H W Wilson Co.*)

library word throughout the world. The UNESCO Public Library Manifesto is an important document, significant at local as well as at international level. Also, through its *Bulletin for Libraries*[6], and library consultancy programmes, UNESCO has been especially influential in promoting libraries in the less-developed parts of the world. The British Council, not the least through its own library services and public library development programmes, has done much to promote the image of the British library profession. In addition, public librarians in Britain and other parts of the world have benefited from the British Council's exchange and education activities.

International relations of this kind may not appear to be immediately relevant to the work of the average public librarian. However, in the long run, such activities, whether at the individual or organizational level, can have a profound effect on the practice and perception of librarianship throughout the world.

NOTES AND REFERENCES

1 McCrae, G 'Paying for the basics', *Lib. Ass Rec.* 79 (3), March 1977.
2 Thorsen, L *Public libraries in Denmark,* Det Danske Selskab, 1972.
3 Metcalf, V 'Bookbang — damp squibs', Letter in *Assistant Librarian* 64 (7), July 1971.
4 See report in *Library Journal* 97 (16), 15 September, 1972.
5 Murison, W J 'Images and real people', *New Library World* 76 (904), October 1975.
6 In January 1979 the *Unesco Bulletin for Libraries* was superseded by the *Unesco Journal of Information Science, Librarianship and Archives Administration.*

Postscript

'New things are made familiar, and familiar things are made new.' Dr Johnson's pronouncement on the poetry of Pope is also an apt summary of the role of library public relations. One of the major functions of public relations is to remind people of the very familiar, and public libraries are very familiar institutions indeed. So common are they, that it is too easy for them to be taken for granted. Yet, few organizations have the capacity to contribute so much to the development of an informed, democratic, and civilized society. PR can help remind legislators and laymen alike of that fact.

For those new to them, public libraries can sometimes be a little daunting, even frightening. Public relations techniques can help make the new and frightening, friendly and familiar.

In a world where the media constantly sing the praises of many less worthy causes, the library song also needs to be heard. There is no reason why commercial concerns should have a monopoly of all the good tunes. Library public relations is, of course, relevant to all types of library but it is my view that there are no more important or challenging library publics than those served by public libraries.

As we move into the post-industrial society, so institutions that provide for the communication of information and ideas become more rather than less important. As populist politicians promote the laws of the economic jungle, so there is an increased need for institutions that stand for the values of an equitable, civilized, and caring society. As the means of communication become concentrated in fewer and fewer hands, so there is an increased need for institutions that provide a wide range of information and ideas. We believe that public libraries are such institutions. At a time when they, like other public services, are under attack, there can be few more important tasks for library managers than to demonstrate and communicate that belief effectively.

John Cotton Dana Award flyer cover. (*H W Wilson Co.*)

Select Bibliography

With a few exceptions the books and articles listed below have been selected from material published in the last ten years. All the items have proved of use in the teaching and/or practice of library public relations.

Public Relations: General Works

Black, S *Practical public relations* 3rd ed., Pitman, 1970.
Black, S *The role of public relations in management,* Pitman, 1972.
Bowman, P & Ellis, N *Manual of public relations,* Heinemann, 1969.
Lesly, P *Lesly's public relations handbook,* Prentice Hall, 1971.

Library Public Relations: General Works

Angoff, A *Public relations for libraries,* Greenwood Press, 1973.
Barrow, P 'Public relations starts at home', *Ontario Library Review* 59, September 1975.
Berry, J 'The Selling of the Library', *Library Journal* 99 (2), 15 January 1974.
Edsall, M S *Library promotion handbook*, Mansell, 1980.
Elliott, C A *Library publicity and service,* Grafton, 1951.
Fontaine, S 'Library public relations: a comment', *Catholic Library World* 46 (7), February 1975.
Fontaine, S *PR Tick/click* American Library Association, 1976. (A half-hour tape-slide presentation.)
Frankenfield, P 'The theory conscious library and the practical community', *Catholic Library World* 46 (10), May/June 1975.
Glazer, F 'Selling the Library', *Library Journal* 99 (11), 1 June 1974.
Greenwood, T *Free public libraries* 2nd ed., Simpkin & Marshall, 1887. (Of great historical interest. Greenwood saw 'the educating of public opinion' as 'the most important part of my entire effort'.)
Harris, W B 'Public relations for public libraries', *Assistant Librarian* 64 (2), February 1971.

Harrison, K C *Public relations for librarians,* Deutsch, 1973.

Hemphill, M 'Communication: Establishing good public relations', *Illinois Libraries,* 55, January 1973.

'Libraries advised against too little PR too late', *Lib. Ass. Rec.* 78 (9), September 1976.

Liebenow, E 'Library public relations: needed service or expensive frill?' *Pacific Northwest Library Association Quarterly* 39, July 1975.

Moore, L A 'Trends, innovations and strategies in library public relations', *Catholic Library World* 46 (10), May–June 1975.

Moran, I (comp.) *The library public relations recipe book,* Public Relations Section, Library Administration Division, American Library Association, 1978. (A useful 'how to' that also contains a very full bibliography which is particularly strong in American material.)

Murphy, E 'Effective communication', *Illinois Libraries* 85, January 1973.

Norton, A 'Why does a public library need public relations?' *Catholic Library World* 48 (7), February 1977.

Ohio Media Spectrum, May 1977. (Special issue on public relations.)

Perkinson, G E 'If truth be told . . . some reflections on the functions of library public relations', *Catholic Library World* 46 (7), February 1975.

'Proceedings of the public relations work-shop', *Drexel Library Quarterly* 1 (1), January 1965.

Raffin, M R & Passmore, R (eds.) *The information worker: identity image and potential,* ASLIB 1977.

Renborg, G *Bibliotekens PR — och kontaktarbete* (Public relations work for libraries), Bibliotekstganst, Lund Berlings, Lund 1977. (Contains English summary.)

Rice, B *Public relations for public libraries,* H W Wilson Co., 1972.

Scilken, M 'Realism in public library public relations', *Library Journal* 97 (7), 1 April 1972.

Usherwood, R C 'Library public relations: an introduction' in Holroyd, G. (ed.) *Studies in library management, Vol. Two,* Bingley, 1974.

'A walking contradiction — the library image', *Assistant Librarian* 65 (12), December 1972.

Weisenberg, C M 'Library PR: a background glance', *Wilson Library Bulletin* 45 (4), December 1970.

Whatley, A 'The untapped market for the public library: a survey', *Lib. Ass. Rec.* 80 (9), 1978.

Williams, G W & Wood, A J 'The image of the librarian', *New Lib. World* 75 (890), August 1974.

Library Public Relations — Ideas and Methods

Baeckler, V V W *PR for pennies. Low cost library public relations,* Sources, 1978.

Baeckler, V V W & Larson L *Go, pep and pop: 250 tested ideas for lively libraries,* Unabashed Librarian, 1976.

Carey, R J P *Library guiding,* Bingley, 1974.

Charlesworth, R 'Saving our souls' *Lib. Ass. Rec.* 80 (2), February 1978. (Report of an experiment in user education.)

Cole, A 'Books, boats and bookweek', *Assistant Librarian* 66 (2), February 1973.

Coleridge, G 'The Bedford Square Bookbang', *Assistant Librarian* 64 (5), May 1971.

Cronin, B 'To be is to be seen', *New Library World* 81 (957), March 1980. (Concerned with the library's visual identity.)

Dove, J 'Libraries and local radio', *Assistant Librarian* 64 (6), June 1971.

Ellis, Vivienne *Lively libraries,* Australian Library Promotion Council, 1975.

Field, R 'The library as publisher', *Lib. Ass. Rec.* 81 (8), August 1979.

Freeman, L & Cossey, C 'Design for identity. Creating the right image', *Municipal and public services journal* 7, December 1973. (Concerned with local authorities in general.)

Gavryck, J *and* Peabody, R 'Shaping the library's in-house publications policy', *Wilson Library Bulletin* 54 (4), December 1979.

Jones, C S (ed.) *Public Library information and referral service,* Gaylord Bros, 1978 (Chapter VII 'Letting people know: public relations and publicity'.)

McNeely, K 'Public relations in the library', *Idaho Librarian* (27), January 1975. (How to write news releases and public service announcements.)

Merrill, R 'Public service broadcasting and libraries', *Wilson Library Bulletin* 53 (6), February 1979.

Murison, W J 'Library users' consultations' in *Proceeding of the Public Library Authorities Conference 1980,* Public Libraries Group of the Library Association, 1980.

Murison, W J, *Public Library users' consultative councils,* Report No. 5499, British Library, 1979.

O'Donnell, P 'Ways in which librarians can inform the public about services and resources', *Wyoming Library Roundup* 28, June 1973.

O'Rourke, E 'Display inside the library', *Assistant Librarian* 68 (1),

January 1975.
Orton, I 'The library as publisher', *Assistant Librarian* 73 (5), May 1980.
Parikh, N 'Organizing for political change', *Library Journal* 105(12), 15 June 1980. (Lobbying techniques.)
Parker, F 'Fifteen fireballs', *Michigan Librarian* 39, Autumn 1973. (Some Michigan methods.)
Phelps, T 'PR Design and community response', *Pacific Northwest Library Association Quarterly* 36, Summer 1972.
Pollet, D 'You can get there from here: new directions in library signage', *Wilson Library Bulletin* 50 (6), February 1976. (Graphics, signposting and colour coding.)
'PR: Where it's at in Michigan Libraries', *Michigan Librarian,* Summer 1973.
Renborg, G 'Public relations activities for the Stockholm City Library', *Scandinavian Public Library Quarterly* 3 (1), 1970.
Sherman, S *ABC's of Library promotion,* Scarecrow, 1971.
Stiles, F 'Action, how to get it started: Effective public relations techniques', *Iowa Library Quarterly* 21, July 1972.
Swan, J 'New visibility for the small library', *Wilson Library Bulletin* 51 (5), January 1977.
Wallick, C H *Looking for ideas? A display manual for libraries and bookstores,* Scarecrow Press, 1970.

Library Public Relations: Management Implications

Baughman, J 'The invisible director', *Library Journal* 105 (12), 15 June 1980. (Advocates 'public activism to achieve the public purpose of the library'.)
Berger, P 'An investigation of the relationship between public relations activities and budget allocation in public libraries', *Information Processing & Management* 15 (4), 1979.
Darling, M 'PR Inservice training', *Unabashed Librarian* 12, Summer 1974.
Gallagher, A 'Publicity in depth', *New Library World* 73 (869) November 1972. (Particularly concerned with the need for PR expertise on library staffs.)
Holliday, S C *The reader and the bookish manner,* illus. by G W Harris, AAL, 1953 (Based on an ALA publication *Patrons are people* this AAL 'classic' although dated is still worth reading. A useful and

painless training text for new members of staff.)

Kies, C *Problems in library public relations*, Bowker, 1974. (A useful collection of case studies.)

Marchant, M 'Public relations and library power', *Idaho Librarian* 25, July 1973.

Savage, E A *The Librarian and his committee*, Grafton, 1942.

Starry, M 'Effective library promotion builds better financial support', *Pacific Northwest Library Association Quarterly* 38, July 1974.

Usherwood, R C 'Public relations', *Libr. Ass. Rec.* 82(4), April 1980. (The PRLG 'value statement'.)

Index

action groups 129
Adel Public Library (USA) 173
advertisements, librarians in 13, 189
advertising 6, 34–6, 195
Alexandria, library of 15
Allison, John 20–2
American Council on Library
    Resources 113
American Library Association 36,
    82, 98, 159
  and advertisements 189
  promotion by 182, 183
  Public Relations Section 188, 191
Annan Report on Broadcasting 70,
    82
annual reports 24–7
Argyle, Michael 119, 120
Argyris, C 118
Aslib/IIS/LA Joint Conference 101
Associated Television
    Corporation 78
Association of Assistant
    Librarians 181, 191
Association of County Councils 152,
    179
Association of London Chief
    Librarians 101
Association of Municipal
    Authorities 152, 179
attitudes
  and communication 114–15,
    120–1, 122
  influencing 3–4, 10
  of library staff 157, 161–2
  of public to libraries 126–7
audio-visual presentations 37–46
  discs (records) 45
  films 42–5
  tape-slide 37–42

awards 191
  John Cotton Dana Awards 36,
    191, 192, 195
awareness of library services 11

badges 98
Bains Report 157
balloons 98, 99
Bedford Square Bookbang 189
Bedfordshire County Library 136
behaviour, non-verbal 119–22
  defence mechanisms 116
Berelson, Bernard 166
Bernays, Edward 5, 6
Berry, John 14
Best Sellers (TV programme) 172
Birmingham Public Library 75, 76,
    77
Birmingham University, INLOGOV
    report 140–1
book jackets 53
booklists 29–30
bookmobiles 104, 105
Books and Beyond (film) 42–3
Booksellers Association 187, 188
Brent 103
British Broadcasting Corporation
  local radio stations 69–70, 71, 75,
    78
  see also television
British Council 43, 193
British Direct Mail Advertising
    Association 103
British Library
  'Need to Know' project 135–6
  Research and Development
    Department 172–3
Brooklyn Public Library 50, 81
Bryan, Carol 47, 55–6

Bucks County Library 161
Bulletin for Libraries,
  UNESCO 193
Burrell, T W 175
bus trips 97, 104
buttons 98

Camden Borough 191
  Library 73
campaigns 138–40, 142, 143
  community action groups 129
  evaluating 166, 168–72
  finance 170–2
  lobbies 10, 177–81
Capital Radio 73
carrier bags 98, 100
Carter, President J 87
catalogues 29
celebrities 55, 75, 82, 133–5, 182
Central Office of Information 44
chairpersons 140–1, 152
Cheshire (Conn.) Public Library 25–6
Cheshire (England) Libraries and
    Museums 137
children 12, 135–6
  art by 49, 100
  competitions for 99–100
  promoting services for 46, 49, 99, 135–6, 183
  Toy Libraries Association 189, 190
Cincinnati
  Friends' group 132
  Public Library boardroom 148, 149
Cinematograph and Indecent Display
    Bill 179
classification 29–30, 106–7
Cleese, John, Video Arts films 161
closures, library 178
committees 140–52
  legislative 179
  open meetings 150–1
  reports for 145–7, 148
  speaking in 148–9

Commonwealth Library
    Association 191
communications 3–4
  barriers to 114–17
  internal staff 113
  non-verbal 119–22
  telephone 124
  understanding people 117–19, 122
community, local 126–36, 138
  action groups 129
  attitudes to libraries 126–7
  Friends' groups 130–4
  informing 134–6
  knowing 127–8
  participation in 128–30
community liaison officers 135
competitions 99–100
complaints and criticism 123–4, 172
computers 100–1, 122
confidence, creating 14–15
controversy, matters of 184
cookery books, community 134
cooperation, library 101–2
Corbett, E V 140
correspondence 102–3
  campaigns 139, 179–81
  in local press 66–7
  stationery 20–2
  see also direct mail
costs
  of public relations 161–2
  of publications 31
Council for Educational
    Technology 42, 46
Council of the Institute of Public
    Relations 6
councils, local 138, 140–52
  committees 144–52
  perks 152
Coventry, City of, Libraries
  'Aids to Library Education' 36
  computer use 100
  news release 61
criticism of library service 172

Index

complaints 123–4
Cronin, Blaise 103
Cumbria County Library 137
cuts in public expenditure, 10, 171, 178

Dana, John Cotton 191
  awards 36, 191, 192, 195
Danish Library Association 182–4
Darcy, B and Ohri, A *Libraries are ours* 129
deaf 131–3
defence mechanisms 116
Department of Education and Science
  The libraries' choice, report 13, 17, 69
  and Library Association 179
design, graphic 32, 47–9
Detroit Public Library 75
Devon, Friends' Groups 130
direct mail 103, 134–5, 173
  feedback 170
  flexidiscs 45
discs (records) 45, 46
displays 51–5
  away from library 53–4, 134
  book 53
  exhibitions 54–5
  mounting 52
  types 51
Donaldson, Lord 10
dress 121

East Sussex County Library 107
Effective Library, The (Hillingdon Report) 126
Eisner, Joseph 29, 134–5
Enquire within (radio programme) 75
ethnic minorities 76, 135
  language 32, 33, 49–50, 76, 77, 81
evaluating public relations 166–76
  economic indications 170–2
  research 172–6
Exchange & Mart 98

exhibitions 54–5
  see also displays
expenditure, public, cuts in 10, 171, 178

Fédération Internationale de Documentation 191
fees for library borrowings 11, 177
female staff 55
films 42–5
Finer, H *English local government* 151
flexidiscs 45, 46
Fontaine, Sue, 113, 173
Frankenberg, R 128
free samples 104
Friends' groups 130–4, 138–9
funding for libraries 9–11, 170–1
  memorial 104–6
fund-raising 131, 132, 171
  campaigns 139–40, 142, 143, 172

Glasgow, Alex 127
Glasgow, community action group 129
Glazer, Frederick 10, 155
government 10
  local councils 138, 140–52
  parliamentary lobbying 177–81
Gowers, Sir Ernest 102
graphic art 47–50, 148
Greenwood, R, INLOGOV report 140–1
Greenwood, Thomas 111
guided tours 107–10
guides, library 27–9, 160
guiding 49, 50

Hampshire County Library 75
Hargreaves, Roger 13
Harris, Bill Best 10
Harrison, K C 42
Hertfordshire County Library 24
Hillingdon Report, *The effective library* 126

204 *The Visible Library*

Humberside, BBC Radio   75

image   11–13, 47–8
Independent Broadcasting
    Authority   70
Independent Local Radio
    stations   70, 71
influence   4–5, 10
information campaigns   168
internal
    communications   113–17
    public relations   13–14
International Federation of Library
    Associations   191
International Public Relations
    Association   5
international relations   191–3
Islington, London Borough of   52,
    191

jackets, book   53
Jackson County Public Library   132
Jarvis, Howard   10
John Cotton Dana Library PR
    Awards   36, 191, 192, 195
Johnson, Dr Samuel   194

Kanawha Public Library   99
Kelly, George   134
Kitt, Eartha   75

Lambeth, London Borough of
    advice on reports   145
    committee   152
    letters sent   20–2, 102–3
    PR Department   158
    publications   30, 148
language   32
    of ethnic minorities   32, 33, 49–50,
        76, 77, 81
Law Society   186
Leicestershire   135, 159
letter-writing   102–3
    campaigns   139, 179–81
    local press   66–7

stationery   20–2
see also direct mail
Lewisham libraries   172
Librarians' Anti-Defamation
    League   189
Libraries are ours   129
Libraries choice, The (DES
    Report)   13, 17, 69
Libraries Open and Free   180
Library Association   5, 26, 28–9, 49,
    147
    and members   181–2
    need for PRO   185–8
    political action by   177–81
    promotion by   182–5
    publicity materials in library of   36
Library User Councils   130
lists of library material   29–30
livery   14, 104
lobbies   10, 177–81
    see also campaigns
local authorities
    councils   138, 140–52
    PR departments   14–15, 157–8
    staff   13–14
    see also councils, local *and names of
        authorities*
local communities *see* community,
    local
Local Government Act, 1972   150
local organizations *see* organizations,
    local
Local Radio Councils   130
local radio *see* radio
local studies   30, 148
London Weekend Television   101
Lyons, J   120

McClellan, A W   107
McCrae, G   181
McGarry, K J   175
McIntyre, Robert B   3
management
    corporate   140–1, 158
    library   122–5

staff, library 115–19
 of public relations 157–64
 see also committees *and* councils
Manchester Public Libraries 107
 tours 108, 109
Maud Report, HMSO 157
membership, control of library 162
memorials 104–6, 132
minorities *see* ethnic minorities
Morris, Desmond 119
Muggeridge, Malcolm 5
Murison, William J 130, 137, 189

Nabisco Company 189
Nassau Library System 98
National Book League 187, 188
National Book Week, 1972 104, 185, 189
National Consumer Council 137
National Library Week 185, 189
Neale, Cherie 40, 41
New York Public Library
 Budget Action Handbook 138
 film 43–4
 fund-raising 171
 Oriental Collection 33, 43
 publicity 33, 61, 170
 radio shows 75
 television 80–2
 tours 108
Newcastle-upon-Tyne Polytechnic 172
news releases 58–65
 distribution 63–4
photos 62
 presentation 60–2
 radio 71
 structure 59–60
 timing 64–5
newsletters 29, 134–5
notices 22–4
Nottingham Public Library 99, 100
 and BBC radio station 69, 75

On the shelf (radio programme) 75, 77

Open University 121
opinion, public 3–4, 10–11
organizations, local 28, 128–9
 displays by 51
 library tours for 108
 promoting library 131–3
 speaking to 28, 45, 86–8
Oriental collection, New York Public Library 33, 43

Parliamentary and Scientific Committee 179
parliamentary lobbying 177–81
payment for libraries 11, 177
perks 152
Perry, Michael 145
Philadelphia, Free Library of
 announcements 61, 79
 Friends' group 131–4
 Old Philadelphia 30
 Public Relations Department 67
 Super Sunday 102
photography 41
 films 42–5
 for press releases 62
 slides 39
 see also tape-slide presentations
Pinter, Harold 116
Plainedge Public Library 29, 134
planning public relations 163–4
Plymouth City Library 10
Poland 53
political action 138–40
political public relations 10, 177–81, 187
posters 24, 101
 American Library Association 182, 183
 competition design 99, 100
 examples 35, 100, 178, 180, 183
press 57–68
 conferences 65–6
 contact 65–8
 cuttings 148, 149, 167–8
 features 67–8
 letters 66–7

releases *see* news releases
pressure groups   129
  lobbies   10, 177–81
  see also campaigns
printers   31
Proposition 13 (USA)   10
Public Lending Right   177
Public Libraries Research Group, statement on library public relations   174–5
public opinion   3
Public Relations Society of America   6
Public Relations Departments
  ALA   188, 191
  LA, need for   185–8
  library   159
  local authority   14, 157–8
public relations
  community   126–36
  definition of   6–7
  evaluating   166–76
  function of   3–5, 194
  image   5
  for libraries   9–15, 177–92, 193–5
  managing, for libraries   157–64
  planning   163–4
  research into   172–6
Public Service Announcements   78–82, 169
publications   19–36
  audio-visual   37–46
  cooperative   101
  cost   31
  design   47–50
  distribution   34, 134
  frequency   32–4
  production   31–2
Publishers Association   187, 188
Publishers Publicity Circle   188
Pyke, Magnus   92

radio   69–82
  advance publicity for   76–8, 81
  ALA provision for   182
  evaluating coverage   83–4, 168
  libraries on   71–6
  local stations   69–70
  Public Service Announcements   78–82, 169
Readers Digest   45
records (discs)   35, 45, 46
Rediffusion Television   172
releases *see* news releases
Renborg, Greta   173
reports
  annual   24–7
  for committees   145–7, 148
research into library promotion   172–6
response, public   170
reviews by community   134
Rice, Betty   82
Roadshow Info (radio programme)   70
Rokeach, Milton   24
rules   28, 161–2
Rummel, Kathleen   159, 163

samples, free   104
Sapir, E   120
Savage, Ernest   1, 141, 144
schools   28, 135–6
Serendipity (National Book League)   104
services, awareness of library   9–11, 14
Sheffield   159
  Libraries Coordinating Committee   101, 160–1
  Public Library, films   42–3
  University   40
Shropshire County   159, 161
Skeffington Report   157
slides   39
  see also tape-slide presentations
slogans   98, 104, 142, 143
smiling   119, 121
Smirnoff Vodka advertisement   13
Society of Young Publishers   188
Somerset, Friends' group   130
South Hackney School   136

Speak for yourself (radio series) 70
speaking, public 86–96
 in committee 148–9
 with film 45
 handout guides 28, 95–6
 microphone 94–5
 preparation 86–9
 presentation 88–93
 question time 93–4
 vote of thanks 94
Spock, Dr Benjamin 92
staff, library 13–14
 attitude to public relations 157
 behaviour 119–25
 communications 113–17
 female 55
 management of 116–19
 new, guide for 28–9
 in reports 26
 training of 96, 108, 160–1
stationery 20–2
status 114
Stiles, F, 'Community relations' 173
stock arrangement 106–7
strikes 119
Suffolk County Library 137
support 6, 10–11
 Friends' groups 130–4, 138–9
surveys 170
Sutton, London Borough of,
    publications 30, 46, 98
Sweden 173

talks *see* speaking, public
tape-slide presentations 37–42
 checklist 40–1
 presentation 42
 script 37–9, 40
 slides 39
telephone
 campaigns 140
 listing 107
 techniques 124–5
television 69, 82–3, 101
 appearing on 82–3
 evaluating coverage 83–4, 168

Public Service
 Announcements 78–82, 169
 Videotex services 101
Thebes, library of 15
ties, library 142
Totterdell, B and Bird, J The
    Hillingdon Report 126
tours
 coach 97
 library 107–10, 160·
Toy Libraries Association 189
 comic 190
trade unions 160
training staff 96, 108
 in public relations 160–1
transport, library 104, 105

UNESCO 193

values 115–16
volunteers
 advisory bodies 130
 tour guides 108, 160

Wandsworth Council 153
West Virginia Library Commission
 balloons 99
 campaigns 140, 142, 143
 Friends 132
 fund-raising 10, 104–6
 presentation to Governor's
    Conference 37
 publications 28
 transport 104, 105
Westminster 135, 172
Whitford Committee on
    Copyright 179
Williams Committee on obscenity
    law 179
Wilson Company, H W 191, 195
Wilson Library Bulletin 51
women staff 55

Yates Committee on recreation
    management 179
Youth Libraries Group 181